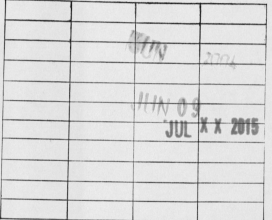
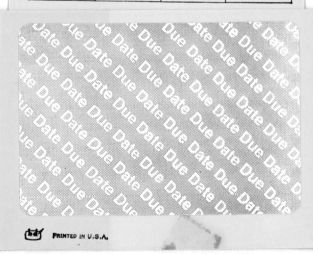

THE FOLKLORE SOCIETY

MISTLETOE SERIES

Ballad Studies

BALLAD STUDIES

edited by E.B.Lyle

Published by D.S.Brewer Ltd

and Rowman and Littlefield

for The Folklore Society

1976

77- 187

6. 'Miss Reburn's Ballads: A Nineteenth-Century Repertoire from Ireland' (c) Alisoun Gardner-Medwin 1976.

Other articles in this book are copyright as first printed.

Published by D.S.Brewer Ltd.
240 Hills Road Cambridge
and P.O.Box 24 Ipswich IP1 1JJ

ISBN (UK) 0 85991 020 2
ISBN (USA) 0-87471-898-8

First published in the U.S.A. 1976 by
Rowman and Littlefield Totowa N.J.

Printed and bound in Great Britain by
Redwood Burn Limited, Trowbridge & Esher

CONTENTS

ACKNOWLEDGEMENTS

'When Is a Poem Like a Sunset?' by J.M.Sinclair
first appeared in *A Review of English Literature*
6 (1965) 76-91, 'History and Harlaw' by David
Buchan in the *Journal of the Folklore Institute* 5
(1968) 58-67, '*The Wee Wee Man* and *Als Y Yod on ay
Mounday*' by E.B.Lyle in *Scottish Literary News* 3
(1973) 21-9 and '*The Grey Selkie*' by Alan Bruford
in *Scottish Studies* 18 (1974) 63-81. These four
articles are reprinted here by kind permission of
the editors of these journals. 'The Scottish Element in Traditional Ballads Collected in America'
by Herschel Gower is a revised form of the article
'The Scottish Palimpsest in Traditional Ballads
Collected in America' in *Reality and Myth: Essays
in American Literature in Memory of Richmond Croom
Beatty* ed. William E.Walker and Robert L.Welker
(Nashville, 1964) 117-44 and appears here by kind
permission of Vanderbilt University Press. For
permission to reprint 'Popular Ballad and Medieval
Romance' by Holger Olof Nygard which appeared in
*Folklore International: Essays in Honor of Wayland
Debs Hand* ed. D.K.Wilgus (Hatboro, Pa., 1967) 161-
73 we are indebted to the Gale Research Company.
'*The Grey Cock*: Dawn Song or Revenant Ballad?' by
Hugh Shields is a revised and extended treatment
of a subject handled in 'Une *Alba* dans la Poésie
Populaire Anglaise?', *Revue des Langues Romanes*
79 (1971) 461-75. 'Miss Reburn's Ballads: A Nine-
teenth-Century Repertoire from Ireland' by Alisoun
Gardner-Medwin has not appeared elsewhere.

PREFACE

A FINE VOLUME called *The Critics and the Ballad*
edited by MacEdward Leach and Tristram P.Coffin
(Carbondale, Illinois, 1961) made available a
valuable collection of studies of ballads up to
that date. This much more modest production
carries on from that point and brings together a
small selection of recent work. It is motivated by
the feeling that the study of ballads is a subject
in its own right and that it is one which tends to
be neglected since it spreads beyond the limits of
the chronological periods into which literature is
so often divided.

The first article here clears away some of the
confusions of the early part of this century and
lets us look freshly at the question of the relationship of ballad and medieval romance. Its
author, Professor Holger Olof Nygard of Duke
University, North Carolina, is well known to
ballad scholars for his book *Heer Halewijn* (Hel-
sinki 1958), a study of the international ballad
which appears in Child as No.4 *Lady Isabel and the
Elf Knight*. He suggests in his article that examining specific ballads is likely to be more
valuable than dealing in generalizations and it
does seem to me that the problems posed by individual ballads frequently require much greater scope
than they can receive in the anthology headnotes
where they have often been treated. Accordingly,
each of the four pieces that follow this article
is devoted to a single ballad and I hope that the
findings of concentrated studies such as these may
enable us to move away at last from dependence on
F.J.Child's influential *English and Scottish
Popular Ballads* of nearly a century ago. My own
contribution explores the relationship of the
supernatural ballad *The Wee Wee Man* (Child 38) to
a work found in a fourteenth-century manuscript.
The ballad on the battle of Harlaw (Child 163) and

the event itself are considered by Dr David
Buchan, senior lecturer in English Studies at
Stirling University and author of *The Ballad and
the Folk* (London and Boston 1972), a study of
balladry in the northeast of Scotland which won
the Chicago Folklore Prize in 1973. Dr Alan Bruford, who is archivist at the School of Scottish
Studies in Edinburgh University and author of
Gaelic Folk-Tales and Mediaeval Romances (Dublin
1969), has done extensive field-work in the Orkney
and Shetland Isles and here turns his attention to
The Grey Selkie (Child 113) which has been found
only in these islands. *The Grey Cock* (Child 248)
is put into context by Dr Hugh Shields, lecturer
in French at Trinity College, Dublin, who has combined work in the area of Old French and Anglo-
Norman with an energetic contribution to the study
of Irish ballads as a collector, as an editor of
Irish Folk Music Studies and as author of a number
of articles including a most useful survey of 'Old
British Ballads in Ireland' in *Folk Life* 10 (1972).

Turning from studies of single ballads, we then
have a survey of an individual's repertoire of
songs, set down in America but of Irish origin.
This material from Child's papers in the Houghton
Library, Harvard, which has not previously been
printed, is presented by Alisoun Gardner-Medwin,
whose publications include 'The Ancestry of *The
House Carpenter*: A Study of the Family History of
the American Forms of Child 243' in the *Journal of
American Folklore* 84 (1971), and who is at present
concentrating on Scottish-Danish relationships
among ballads. Professor Herschel Gower of Vanderbilt University, Nashville, Tennessee, takes a
broader sweep in the next article which deals with
some of the ballads collected from oral tradition
in the United States of America. Professor Gower
combines interests in literature, history and
folklore and his publications include an edition
of *The Hawk's Done Gone and Other Stories* (Nash-

ville 1968) and a series of joint articles with
James Porter in *Scottish Studies* on the song
repertoire of Jeannie Robertson. Finally we have a
study in which J.M.Sinclair, Professor of Modern
English Language at the University of Birmingham,
brings his specialist skill to bear on a familiar
literary ballad in a 'laboratory' situation. He
has published *A Course in Spoken English: Grammar*
(London 1972) and, with R.M.Coulthard, a monograph
called *Towards an Analysis of Discourse: The English used by teachers and pupils* (London 1975).

I should like to express my thanks to all the
contributors for allowing this book to be put
together and to the Folklore Society for including
it in the Mistletoe series. I am also grateful to
P.N.Shuldham-Shaw for preparing the music for
publication.

E.B.LYLE

School of Scottish Studies
University of Edinburgh

1. POPULAR BALLAD AND MEDIEVAL ROMANCE

Holger Olof Nygard

THE QUESTION OF the relations of the ballads and
medieval romances touches upon the great contro-
versy which created such a flurry in ballad criticism during the early years of this century. There
were two firmly held and forcefully expressed extremes between which ranged a wide array of more
considered opinion. The extremes were composed, on
the one hand, of communalists, who held that
ballads originated from the spontaneous song of
the throng or communal group in dance or cel-
ebration of some event, and, on the other, of
scholars who viewed ballads as the degeneration of
the minstrelsy of romance in the later Middle Ages.
The shades of opinion between these two extremes
reflected measures of caution and prudence, for
the evidence existent was hardly sufficient to enable anyone to generalise in a bold and forthright
manner. The central issue in the Ballad War is now
a matter of history, well documented, analysed and
laid to rest,[1] as is apparent from a review of the
names and dates of the contestants in the squabble.
But the particularities of interdependence between
the popular ballads of the late Middle Ages and
such forms as the courtly lyric, the carol, religious song, saga and Eddic material, folk-tales,
historical chronicles, and particularly verse romances, have by no means been agreed upon. How the
ballads interrelate with these other genres remains an intriguing line of investigation for the
balladist pursuing questions of genesis and development of the form or attempting to define and
compare these various genres.

In his highly respected handbook to the ballad
of tradition, G.H.Gerould completely skirts the
question of ballad-romance relationship. The
following equivocal remark is his most direct
statement on the matter: 'Some of the exploits of

1

ballad heroes have much in common with the ex-
travagances attributed to the knights of medieval
romance.'[2] He deduces no indebtedness from one
form to the other. About an allied question he
sees no advantage in continuing 'the intermittent
warfare that has been carried on for more than a
century by communalists and individualists. Could
the truth be reached along those lines, there
would have been peace between the combatants ere
this.'[3] There is little chance of resolving the
questions finally as to whether or not ballads
derived ultimately from medieval romances, or
whether the two forms represent parallel streams
whose waters blended for a time. The romance relations of only certain individual ballads can be
discussed with any profit, and even here much of
what can be said must remain conjectural and would
take on appearances of the major contention all
over again in little. Contention there has been;
most of the great names in ballad criticism have
contributed to it, either with sweeping assertions
or with sporadic jabs while en route elsewhere.

There are many and varying cases for and against
the romances as the source of the ballads. It must
be made clear at the outset that all scholars must
perforce agree that a few ballads are derived from
romances; the evidence is to all appearances too
conclusive for anyone to think otherwise, although
the intermediary steps in the transition from
romance to ballad, or the act of recreation of a
romance in ballad form is lost, as with most processes of oral tradition, past reclaiming. The
contention centred on the general question: Are
ballads as a genre derived by a process of degeneration (the pejorative view) or by a process of
reduction (less damaging to the respectability of
the ballad as a form) from the medieval romances,
or have they as a genre sprung up spontaneously or
from models of poetry or song other than the romances? Another manner of phrasing the question

would be: Were the ballads as a genre the work of professional ballad-makers or minstrels, or were they as a class the fortuitous, natural growth of a poetic mode of expression amongst unsophisticated people loosely termed the folk? That the minstrels made some ballads and that they were the purveyors of many no one has disputed or will dispute. But what of the origins? Were they by way of the romances or not?

Professor Child's knowledge of the relation of ballads and romances was as complete as any one's has ever been; it is a pity that we have from his pen no more than the *obiter dicta* in his headnotes to the separate ballads. As he never expressed his total view of the ballads and their origins in an organised and systematic essay (for the *Johnson's Universal Cyclopaedia* article is not to be 'regarded as final'), we are left judging his views as they occur here and there among the headnotes in his final collection. Two important conclusions can be drawn from them: in the first place he was non-committal, and in the second place, to the degree that he did reveal his thoughts on the subject, his remarks do not under close scrutiny retain a consistency of view. His hesitating to formulate sweeping conclusions would appear to be part of the circumspection, as with Gerould, that Child exercised in his study of the ballads.[4] This circumspection as to the matter of priority of tale, chronicle, romance, or ballad is forcefully put in his headnote to *Sir Aldingar* (59), the chief incident of which is widely paralleled in the other forms.[5] Child observes:

There is little or nothing in all these tales that can be historically authenticated, and much that is in plain contradiction with history. Putting history out of the question, there is no footing firmer than air for him who would essay to trace the order of development. Even if we

3

exaggerate the poverty of human invention so
far as to assume that there must have been a
single source for stories so numerous and so
diversified in the details, a single exposition
of the subject-matter, with subordinate connections seems all that is safe, at present, to
attempt.[6]

Sir Aldingar is possessed of so many parallels in
chronicle (back to William of Malmesbury), historical facts, romances, and continental ballads, that
this ballad invites speculation as to which of the
forms came first. 'Grundtvig,' as Child tells us,
'admitting that the time has not come for anything
more, sketches an hypothesis of the evolution and
transmission of the story, "as a mere experiment."'[7] Again, in Child's introduction to *Earl
Brand* (7), concerning the familiar ballad commonplace of plants which spring from the graves of
lovers, he writes:

The idea of the love-animated plants has been
thought to be derived from the romance of
Tristan, where it occurs; agreeably to a general
principle, somewhat hastily assumed, that when
romances and popular ballads have anything in
common, priority belongs to the romances. The
question as to precedence in this instance is an
open one, for the fundamental conception is not
less a favourite with ancient Greek than with
medieval imagination.[8]

Child notes that the story of *Fair Annie* (62), as
with those of many other ballads, has been told
elsewhere, in this case in a lay by Marie de
France, *Le Lai del Freisne*. More hasty judgments
would attribute the ballad to the lay source, for
the tale, of Breton origin, 'is 300 years older
than any manuscript of the ballad.' But Child
remarks:

Comparison will quickly show that it is not the

4

source either of the English or of the Low German and Scandinavian ballad. The tale and the ballads have a common source, which lies further back, and too far for us to find.[9]

Professor Walter Morris Hart, in his attempt to reduce Child's remarks about specific ballads into a consistent statement about all ballads, points out that Child regarded them as examples of 'a distinct species of poetry which preceded the poetry of art,...the product of a homogeneous people.'[10] Hart may well have been pushing his own view of the matter in attributing to the ballads a popular origin, for he draws Child's statement of opinion from the *Johnson's Universal Cyclopaedia* article, in which Child brings himself to say that the ballad's 'historical and natural place is anterior to the appearance of the poetry of art, to which it has formed a step, and by which it has been regularly displaced, and in some cases all but extinguished.'[11] This statement is certainly not consistent with Child's later view that 'the ballad is not originally the product or the property of the common orders of the people,' a statement that the anti-communalists made much of.[12] Even Hart quotes Child to the effect that the ballad 'is at its best when it is early caught and fixed in print,' the implicit suggestion being that the haphazard process of oral transmission produces in all probability a mutilated and degenerate specimen. What is more, Child gives direct support to the 'romance' and the 'minstrel' theory of origins in the case of a number of individual ballads. He recognises that *The Lochmaben Harper* (192) has 'the genuine ring of the best days of minstrelsy'; that *The Rising in the North* (175) is 'the work of a loyal but unsympathetic minstrel'; and that *Crow and Pie* (111) is 'not a purely popular ballad, but rather of the kind which for convenience may be called a minstrel ballad.' Of *The Boy and the Mantle* (29), *King Arthur and King Cornwall* (30), and *The Marriage of Sir Gawain* (31), he writes:

> They would come down by professional rather than domestic tradition, through mintrels rather than knitters or weavers. They suit the hall better than the bower, the tavern or public square better than the cottage, and would not go to the spinning-wheel at all.[13]

Finally, he makes a direct assertion which so much appears to favour the 'degeneracy' theory of the ballad that it must have worried the communalists. The assertion is that

> Nothing...is more obvious than that many of the ballads of the now most refined nations had their origin in that class whose acts and fortunes they depict —the upper class— though the growth of civilization has driven them from the memory of the highly polished and instructed and has left them as an exclusive possession of the uneducated.[14]

It is apparent that Child's chance remarks among the many pages he wrote about specific ballads may be rifled for grist for any partisan mill.

Let us now turn to the partisans.

Eschewing chronology, we turn first to two of Child's close followers, George Lyman Kittredge and Francis B.Gummere. They (particularly Gummere) speak for the 'communalists'. In his Introduction to the Abridged Edition of the Child collection, which appeared in 1904, Kittredge stated the communal theory, but rather more guardedly than Gummere. Kittredge described by picturesque stages 'the supposedly inconceivable phenomenon of a unanimous throng composing poetry with one voice.'[15] He has little to say of romance origins, but he recognises, following Child, that the minstrel

pieces 'stand in close relation to the materials
of mediaeval romantic fiction, even if they are
not directly derived from metrical romances.' In
writing of Peter Buchan's texts, those supplied by
James Rankin, he describes them as the work in
effect of 'a professional minstrel of the humbler
order, or at least the lineal descendant or representative of the minstrel class of former times.'
By comparing the reworkings of James Rankin with
the ballads being collected in the early nineteenth century from non-professional sources he
sees

> in a moment the absurdity of the notion that our
> popular ballads were composed or even largely
> transmitted by minstrels. And thus one chapter,
> and a troublesome one, of our investigation is
> brought to a satisfactory close.

Kittredge closes his Introduction with the assur-
ance that ballads are not of romance and minstrel
origin; the assertion looks back to his earlier
description of 'the characteristic method of
ballad authorship as improvisation in the presence
of a sympathetic company which may even, at times,
participate in the process.'[16]

Gummere, the far more effusive proponent of the
communal theory of composition, devoted the
efforts of his scholarly life to establishing that
theory. In 1897, in the Introduction to his *Old
English Ballads*, he asserted his belief that
'English ballads could be traced back in an unbroken chain to the primitive Germanic song,'[17]
could be traced back if in fact we had not 'lost
important links of the chain.' The missing links,
'the underground river of balladry,' were clearly
not the romances in Gummere's construct of prob-
abilities. In 1907, in his *Popular Ballad*, he
stated, quite without attempt at proof, that
ballads 'have, as a rule, better claims to priority than the romances can offer.'[18] Gummere was

7

ever reticent about the romance in his many writings. At one point he went so far as to distinguish, in a general way, between the matter of the ballads and that of the romances:

> Theirs [the ballads'] is the romance of tradition, a kind of obsolete reality, as different from literary romance of the past as it is from modern realism. They have not much of the fantastic element so plentiful in popular tales, and speak more willingly of old customs than of old myth.[19]

He grudgingly recognised that certain ballads do derive from romances. *Sir Aldingar* 'derives very superfluously from a romance.' Child described *Hind Horn* (17) as 'the catastrophe of the story related in full in a number of gests and romances'[20] thereby implying priority of the romance. To Gummere, with his evolutionary and developmental notions about ballads, *Hind Horn* as we have it is still a situation ballad to which has accrued a slight touch of explanatory narrative.[21] Gummere believed that the romance was the mere filling out of the original ballad. *King Estmere* (60), like *Sir Cawline* (61), 'may possibly be formed upon a romance in stanzas, which itself was composed from earlier ballads.'[22] *Sir Lionel* (18) 'has kept the older way, and may show the sort of ballad out of which a romance like *Sir Cawline* was made.'[23] The ballads with Arthurian matter Gummere, like Kittredge, admits as ballads only because they are 'composed in the popular style and perpetuated for a time by oral tradition.'[24] But the implicit suggestion is that they are usurpers against ballad rights: they have forced their way from the hall into the bower and hearthside. The mystery of the move inward from tribal throng to kitchen and hearthside he does not explain; he is certain that the lordly hall was never the beginning of the process. Gummere's position is maintained as a

fundamentalist might maintain faith in his revealed religion. There is little of the disin-
terested critic about him.

Our next group of critics to shed their light
upon the question of romance origins of the
ballads believed themselves ruled by right reason.
They are principally W.J.Courthope, G.Gregory
Smith, and T.F.Henderson. Their efforts have been
to establish the ballads as a later and plebeian
form of the medieval romances.

Courthope was the first of these to issue his
pronouncements. In 1895 appeared the first volume
of his *History of English Poetry*, of which
chapter 11 bore the title, 'The Decay of English
Minstrelsy.' He avowedly followed Bishop Percy of
more than a century before in tracing the fall of
the minstrel from a station of respectability as a
purveyor of romances to a lowly station as singer
of ballads to unexalted audiences. With the fall
in social level of the minstrel (Sir Philip Sidney,
ca.1580, for all his admiration of the 'blinde
crouder,' was very patronising), there was also a
fall in the level of his song. By Elizabethan
times the minstrel had declined to the level of
vagabond and actor, as legal decrees of the time
tell us. Courthope believed that the historical
sequence in minstrelsy was from Teutonic epic and
heroic poem (such as *Beowulf* and *Widsith*) to
metrical romance to the 'heroic ballad.' He is by
no means innocent of over-riding his evidence; he
says:

> A practical test of the quality of these late
> literary romances is furnished by the neglect
> with which they were treated by the ballad-makers
> who borrowed so freely from the older legends of
> Arthur and Charlemagne.[25]

One might question the words 'borrowed so freely'.
Secondly, the ballad-makers, it is usually recognised, have not been so critically acute as

Courthope would have them; there is much chaff among the wheat, and there is no reason for believing that the chaff was not coexistent from the beginning with the wheat. Thirdly, the ballads may generally have been older than the romances; hence, only the older romances might have been drawn on for the few 'minstrel ballads'. Courthope's view of ballad origins is expressed in the following statement:

> The English ballads that have come down to us fall naturally into three classes: those which reflect the characteristics of the ancient *chanson de geste*; those which combine the features of the *chanson de geste* and the literary romance; and those which have a purely literary origin in the romance, lay, or *fabliaux*.[26]

His case seems good, if one grants one assumption, that the ballads come after and from the romances. For then one is free to analogise the qualities of the *chanson de geste* with *The Battle of Otterburn* (161); the combined features of *chanson de geste* and literary romance with the Robin Hood ballads; and the literary romances, lays and *fabliaux* with a fair number of ballads like *Sir Aldingar* (69), *Sir Cawline* (61), and *Child Waters* (63). But Courthope does not succeed in proving his thesis. There is no genuine support for his theory in his arbitrarily asserting that among the ballads 'the sentiments, the form, the language, show plain traces of decline.'[27] He merely begs the question. If one held an opposing view (that ballads gave way to romances), one might as easily say that these elements show refinement and elevation in the more sophisticated romances. Courthope sets about, on the basis of being right so far, to prove that *The Battle of Otterburn* is a debased *chanson de geste*, that the Robin Hood cycle is a debased Round Table cycle, and that *Sir Aldingar* and other songs are ballad-

ised romances. For each of these specific categories he makes a beautifully convincing case.
Sir Aldingar and a handful of other ballads are of
course admitted by nearly everyone to be from romance material (although we would do well to recall Child's hesitance here). Robin Hood in the
Gest (117) is masterfully shown to be a demo-
cratising (King Arthur of the Commons, as Gregory
Smith called him) of the noble outlaw Fulke Fitz
Warine of romance, with touches from Arthurian
tales transformed to suit the sentiments of a
meaner audience. But Courthope's argument appears
more sweepingly conclusive than it really is. He
has chosen his examples warily. They admit of the
type of demonstration he needed to establish his
point. Few ballads would serve as well as those he
deals with at length. Very obviously absent are
the international ballads such as *The Twa Sisters*
(10) and *Lady Isabel and the Elf Knight* (4), many
of them early, lacking in metrical and literary
analogues, and inconceivable as extended romances.
Courthope took insufficient account of the spread
of ballads over the European continent. He treated
the question of the ballads as very much an insular problem. Nor did it seem to occur to Courthope that he was describing a very limited number
of them when he assigned their origins to the
degeneration of minstrelsy. Nor did it occur to
him that there might have been admittedly a fair
amount of borrowing of romance materials and
tricks on the part of the ballad singers in order
that they might improve or merely vary a genre
that may have existed separate from and before the
romances. The great fashion which romances certainly enjoyed could account for the tremendous im-
print that they made upon the ballad. Romances had
the sanction of nearly every class, but particularly of the gentry, and it must be admitted that
'the people' have always had an eye for noble
example to follow. But Courthope does overload the

11

evidence of 'degeneracy' in ballads; they are in some cases degenerate, clumsy, and silly, and in others refined, exquisite, and fashioned as if with taste. The medieval romances enjoy the same disparity in degrees of excellence; Chaucer had tried to write the best and worst of them. Once again in criticism of Courthope's views, it does not seem to occur to him that ballads might not be a homogeneous entity, that in reality they might draw their being from a vast variety of sources, even if one limits one's considerations to the stories and details of narration, as Courthope does. The element of song is a facet of ballad form that Courthope neglects completely. A degenerated romance does not blossom forth in song by virtue of the degeneration; something radically different has been added. The melodic aspect would suggest that ballad is a separate genre, distinct and independent of the romance. Finally, Courthope, in 1895, took insufficient notice of the fact that ballad-making was not 'a lost art', as Kittredge called it, that ballads were still being made, even in the English-speaking world, and not from romances. Courthope's case is brilliantly suggestive and right in certain limited respects; it was a powerful corrective to the communal theory so popular about 1900; but as a blanket assertion to cover all ballads, it seems Procrustean.

G.Gregory Smith and T.F.Henderson reasserted the conclusions of Courthope, with little variation. Smith, in *The Transition Period* (1900), tried to show how the prosody of the ballad (neglected by Courthope) evolved, very simply, from the decomposition of the literary romance. He called the ballad 'the literary débris of the Middle Ages,'[28] to go one better than his predecessor. Henderson, while an upholder of the romance origins of the ballad, is much more generous toward the ballad as a form. In his *Ballad in Literature*, 1912, he says:

12

The romance, from which it often borrowed its themes, has now become archaic: the life has gone out of it; but the ballad has laid hold of its essence, and in a condensed form recreated it.[29]

He believes it to be the misfortune of the ballad that it has fallen into the hands of the common people and that it has had to be perpetuated by them:

Its traditional development, in this fashion, could not possibly be other than decadent; it was beyond it to produce anything that could properly be regarded as a new literary creation, but only a kind of mongrel debasement.[30]

In his *Scottish Vernacular Literature, a History*, published as early as 1898, Henderson does modify Courthope's view to some degree. He believes that there are 'a few apparent exceptions [i.e., they are not from romances] in the case of individual ballads'; he believes that Courthope overdoes the idea of 'degeneracy' of the form in the hands of minstrels; and he is willing to consider 'that some of the traditional Scots ballads were originally the work of poets other than minstrels.'[31] Another adherent of the romance origins school who would seek to modify Courthope's views is J.H. Millar. In his *Literary History of Scotland*, 1903, he voices the opinion that 'It would be rash to deny that metrical versions of *Märchen* may have existed at a date considerably prior to the development of the "full dress" romance or epic.'[32] But he holds as a principle the idea that 'The corruption of the minstrel, in effect, is the generation of the ballad-maker,' and that 'a Ballad is more modern than a Romance, though the *Märchen* which forms its subject is much older than the derivative myth with which the Romance deals.'[33] Neither he nor Henderson can establish incontrovertibly

the notion that all ballads are literary deriva-
tions; they rest assured that their view has more
commonsense than that of the communalists, and
that they take 'the ballads as they are — not as
they may have been, or ought to have been.'34 They
neglect to consider that even in the last statement quoted, the word 'ballads' would more fitting-
ly read 'a few of the ballads'. Henderson and
Millar both have an added confidence in their
views because no less a personage than Sir Walter
Scott had said a century before that 'the further
our researches are extended, the more we shall see
ground to believe that the romantic ballads of
later times are, for the most part, abridgements
of the ancient metrical romances, narrated in a
smoother stanza and a more modern language.'35

We finally arrive at the group whose opinions
are similar to Child's, who feel the grounds for
dogmatic opinion insufficiently certain. This
group if not effecting a compromise, at least goes
along partially with both schools of thought. The
first of these critics is Andrew Lang. In his
first writings on the ballads he supported the
communalists, in fact, gave them part reason for
being, with his view of the ballads as 'the im-
memorial inheritance at least of all European
peoples.' His familiarity with folklore and anthro-
pological study made him speak out against Courthope's 'ignorance of the comparative method, and
of the ballad literature of Europe in general.'36
He would 'fain break a lance with Mr.Courthope on
his general doctrine,' advancing his notion that
'In perhaps more numerous cases the popular ballad
does not "reproduce, in a mould peculiar to itself,
the subject-matter of the older gests, romances,
or lays."' Although much of what Lang had said
seems to be of a piece with Gummere's views, yet
the greater caution of Lang led him finally to a
compromise position. We note, for instance, his remark in the Introduction to his *Collection of Ballads*:

14

Thus, when a literary romance and a ballad have the same theme, the ballad may be a popular degradation of the romance; or it may be the original popular shape of it, still remaining in tradition.[37]

The note of compromise is also struck in his *Encyclopaedia Britannica* article of 1910:

It would be an error to suppose that most romantic folk-songs are vulgarizations of literary romance...and the opposite error would be to hold that this process of borrowing from and vulgarization of literary medieval romance never occurred.

Professor W.P.Ker, about the same time, in his British Academy lecture of 1909, effected a similar compromise:

The ballads are not merely a limb of the great medieval body of romance; they are a separate form. They are not mere versified folklore, because their form – the *Idea* of a Ballad –makes them reject some of the most delightful fairy tales as unfit for their poetical scope. They are not degradations of longer stories, for even when they have the same plot, they make a different thing of it.[38]

Ker, allying himself not fully with either school of contention, transferred the emphasis from matter to form; 'Ballad is an Idea, a poetical Form, which can take up any matter, and does not leave the matter as it was before.'[39] The ballad of *King Orfeo* (19), for instance, 'comes, no doubt, from the romance of *King Orfeo*. This is one of the most beautiful of the old rhyming lays; but it does not account for the ballad. There is something in the ballad which has come in another way.'[40]

Since Ker's pronouncements the issue has been

15

rather still. Further contention would be a mere
retreading of the same ground. The difficulty of
the matter lies in the absence of sufficient evidence upon which to base a final opinion. Opinions
have been more prudent since Gummere and Courthope
wrote. As G.Gregory Smith put it — 'The comfort of
the matter to each dogmatist is that in the absence of data it is hard to prove the unreason-
ableness of his view.'[41]

The relations of ballads and the longer forms
of medieval poetry have tantalised students of the
subject from the beginnings of modern scholarship
in the nineteenth century. The question of priority of one genre with respect to another, the
notion of the metaphorically biological development of forms of poetry, the organic concept of
genetic relations of literary forms, loom large in
the history of nineteenth and early twentieth
century studies. It was noted by Scandinavians
that some of their ballads are derived from sagas
and lays of eddic material. Spanish *romançeros* are
historical romances reduced in form to ballads.
Conversely, the Finnish ballads concerning the
mythic figures Väinämöinen and Ilmarinen are the
stuff from which Elias Lönnrot fashioned the epic
Kalevala, only a little more than a century ago,
thus adding vitality to the Homeric debate concerning the *Iliad* and the *Odyssey* as stitched
ballads.

A comparison of a specific ballad with its romance analogues (*Hind Horn* and *King Horn*) in attempting to determine which is antecedent to the
other is a worthwhile enterprise. Even Gummere
recognised that the romance-ballad relationship
might be a two-way process, for he admitted that
minstrels 'could take a good romance and make it
over into indifferent ballads.'[42] But generalisations based on a consideration of the whole
ballad corpus and the body of medieval verse that
might be comprehended by the term romance will not

16

yield us secure results. Courthope proceeded by such a method; if anything, the weight of evidence would lead one to believe him wrong, to doubt that ballads are degenerate minstrelsy. Ballads permit no tone of mystery or vagueness; all is matter-of-fact, a literal transcript of actuality, with little poetic fancy. In romances, on the other hand, greater latitude is allowed the imagination. The most fanciful creatures of balladry, such as fire-breathing fiends and five-headed giants, are found in ballads like *King Arthur and King Cornwall* (30), those more or less related to romances. Such fabulous creatures are not at home in those ballads which seem to be markedly independent of the longer, more diffuse and literary forms. 'Burlow Beanie' in the ballad last named may be a household familiar, a Billy Blind, and yet he appears here as a seven-headed fiend with fiery breath. Dreams in ballads are homely stuff, in contradistinction to dreams in romances. Folklore in the romances is highly transformed; 'the ballads [have] kept more of the original telling of the folk.'[43] The Dane J.C.H.R.Steenstrup points out that Christian dogma and doctrines are alluded to often in rhymed romances but are singularly lacking in the poetry of the folk.[44] Romances are notoriously diffuse and spun-out; they are laden with long descriptions. If ballads are derived from them it is strange that they would have so completely lost these characteristics. As Ker puts it, ballads have escaped the vices of romances, for ballads have coherence.[45] Finally, there is the matter of song, which was not with any certainty part of literary romance. The music, it would appear, would provide a break between the two genres. Degeneration of the romance would hardly account for the element of music in ballads and the lyrical quality of the ballad verse as well. Some ballads were indeed recited, the longer ones, such as *The Gest of Robin Hood* (117); at

17

least, touches of evidence from earlier centuries would lead us to believe so. Perhaps here is evidence of the heterogeneity of the ballad, of even a double strain, minstrelsy of a sort falling in with ballad form already established. But such speculation will not carry us far. General comparison of ballad and romance style and language will not answer our question either. The ballad may have acquired its peculiar characteristics, conciseness, interest in the high-point of the story, matter-of-factness, from the process of oral tradition and the impress of the folk mind. The ballad may have had these characteristics before the romance ever appeared, or it may have evolved to these characteristics from the romance as 'sung' by the people.

The ballads in Child's collection which do admittedly have relations with known metrical romances are not many in number.[46] Nor are they the particular items that will determine the answer to the question at hand. The issue in which Courthope and Gummere served as chief spokesmen concerned the bulk of the ballads, the near-300 items in Child's collection the romance relations of which could only be speculated about. Courthope rather cavalierly treated the genre as a whole as conforming with those few ballads that he saw as derived from romances. Partisanship in the issue is no longer in fashion; the argument is today largely historical. And to question the 'degenerate minstrelsy' theory of the ballad no longer implies an adherence to the communal theory of origins, as it once did.

The confluence of ballad and romance traditions in the later Middle Ages still poses a fascinating question admitting of no ready solution. Knight, hawk, hound, 'fair lady', (the last an echo of the 'Bele ——' of French *caroles* to E.K.Chambers),[47] all suggest the matter of romances, and not the rustic life. A bourgeois romance like *Havelok the*

18

Dane is far more plebeian than the majority of
ballads that are supposed to be of the folk. Con-
tenders in the question have not been satisfied
with claiming merely the inception of balladry as
the change of a few romances into a new form, the
ballad. They are only satisfied with claiming all
ballads as the decadent art of romance. But even
if the figure of the yeomanly Robin Hood originally derived from a romance, one can be certain
that the vast majority of Robin Hood ballads did
not derive from romances. The impetus once provided, a ballad about a popular hero, the process
from there on seems to have been self-generative.
The ballad would seem to be a form which drew
sporadically from the materials of romance as well
as from other genres. But the specific origins, or
transitions from something to the ballad form, are
too obscured by incompleteness of record to permit
one to assign the ballads to degenerate or even
transformed minstrelsy of medieval romance.
Ballads and romances may have existed together,
not independent of one another, but each giving to
the other, each possibly an interest of a different level in the social scale (things like *Havelok*
excepted), but coming together at points. Those
points of mutual concourse it is now next to
impossible for us to determine, nor can we be
certain of the degree of interdependence, or the
order of priority. Meanwhile, the record of the
contention in which Gummere and Courthope were
anchor-men leaves one with the lesson in prudence
that it is better to be certain of the uncertainty
than to be wrong.

2. *THE WEE WEE MAN* AND *ALS Y YOD ON AY MOUNDAY*

E.B.Lyle

SINCE THERE IS very little direct evidence to support the impression that certain of the ballads
and songs recorded from tradition in the eighteenth century and onwards have their roots in the
medieval period, it is all the more vital to give
close attention to those connections that can be
traced, for they may be of interest, not only in
themselves, but as indications of processes at
work which would have a general application to the
question of the lost literature of medieval Scotland. Joseph Ritson, who was the first scholar to
note the resemblance between the ballad *The Wee
Wee Man* (Child No.38) and the narrative introduction to the prophecy *Als Y Yod on ay Mounday*,
recognised that the relationship between these
pieces afforded an exceptional opportunity for
study of the effects of transmission. In his *Scotish Songs* (London, 1794) he comments (I.lxxxii):

> There is one song, or rather the fragment of one,
> which seems to merit particular attention from a
> singular evidence of its origin and antiquity:
> it is inserted in the present collection, under
> the title of *The wee wee man*, and begins:
>   As I was walking all alone.
> The original of this song is extant in a Scotish
> or Northhumbrian poem of Edward the first or
> seconds time, preserved in the British museum,
> and intended to be one day given to the public.[1]
> The two pieces will be found to afford a curious
> proof how poetry is preserved for a succession
> of ages by mere tradition; for though the ima-
> gery or description is nearly the same, the
> words are altogether different; nor, had the
> *Canterbury tales* of Chaucer been preserved to
> the present time in the same manner, would there
> have remained one single word which had fallen

21

from the pen of that venerable bard; they would
have been as completely, though not quite so
elegantly, modernised, as they are by Dryden and
Pope: ...

Ritson calls *The Wee Wee Man* a 'fragment' since
it is shorter than its medieval counterpart, but
the ballad narrative is satisfying as it stands
and could well be complete. The *Als Y Yod* narrative has no additional episodes; its greater
length is accounted for by the presence of passages of conversation and description absent from
the ballad, and while it is possible that this
material was lost during transmission or deliberately omitted, it seems to me that it has the
nature of inessential amplification and that the
narrative of *Als Y Yod* was probably arrived at by
padding out a narrative similar in length to the
ballad. In that case, the most likely relationship
would be not, as Ritson supposed, that *Als Y Yod*
was the 'original' of *The Wee Wee Man*, but that
the two pieces were derived from a lost common
source.

Als Y Yod on ay Mounday, which was apparently
composed in Northumbria, is extant in a single
text written down in the first half of the fourteenth century,[2] but *The Wee Wee Man* occurs in a
number of variants, seven of which are printed by
Child.[3] There are criss-crossings of relationships
among the variants, but they fall basically into
two groups,[4] one containing Child A-C and E-G and
the other containing only D of the Child variants
but also an eighteenth-century variant in the St
Clair MS[5] that is roughly contemporary with Child
A, which was printed by David Herd in 1776.[6] Although the Herd and St Clair MS texts belong to
separate groups, they have a great deal in common
and the following narrative outline, divided according to their eight stanzas, applies to both:
(1) the narrator meets a little man, (2) the

22

little man is described, (3) the little man throws
a stone, (4) the narrator exclaims over this feat
of strength, asks where the little man lives and
is invited to visit his home, (5) the narrator and
the little man travel swiftly together until they
arrive at a place where they see a lady, (6) the
lady's beautiful attendants are mentioned, (7) a
splendid castle is described, (8) as the narrator
is observing ladies dancing, the little man sud-
denly vanishes.

The narrative of *Als Y Yod* is a little over
twice as long as these texts of *The Wee Wee Man*
and has a different distribution of material, with
sixty of its seventy-two lines equivalent to the
first half of the ballad and only twelve equivalent to the second half, as can be seen in the
following table of corresponding passages. *The Wee*
Wee Man stanzas are of four lines and the *Als Y*
Yod stanzas are of eight lines. The first and
second halves of stanzas are indicated by 'a' and
'b' respectively.

THE WEE WEE MAN		*ALS Y YOD*	
stanzas	no.of lines	stanzas	no.of lines
1-2	8	1-4a, 5	36
3	4	4b	4
4	4	6-8a	20
5-8	16	8b-9	12

The first stanza of the ballad is parallel to
lines 1-2 and 4-5 of the medieval work, and, in
the opening stanza of *Als Y Yod* given below,[7]
material that is not roughly comparable is en-
closed in square brackets:

Als y yod on ay Mounday
  Bytwene Wyltinden and Walle,
[Me ane aftere brade waye,]
  Ay litel man y mette withalle;
The leste that ever I sathe, [sothe to say,

23

Oithere in boure, oithere in halle;
His robe was noithere grene na gray,
 Bot alle yt was of riche palle.]

Putting the relevant wording alongside the ballad stanza (Herd 1) we have:

As I was walking all alone
  Between a Water and a Wa'
And there I spyed a wee wee man
  And he was the least that ere I saw.

Als y yod on ay Mounday
  Bytwene Wyltinden and Walle,
Ay litel man y mette withalle;
  The leste that ever I sathe.

It seems to me to be a definite possibility that the *Als Y Yod* narrative was expanded from a work beginning with four lines of this type, like the unelaborate opening of *The Hare* in a fifteenth-century manuscript:

By a forrest as I gan fare,
 Walking al myselven alone,
I herd a mourning of an hare;
 Rewfully she made her mone:...[8]

Some of the language in the first stanza of *Als Y Yod* that is not equivalent to the ballad is notably thin, *e.g.* 'Oithere in boure, oithere in halle;' and the later description of the little man includes a half-stanza that demonstrates the filling out of lines by the crude use of very obvious rhyming tags (4a):

Armes scort, for sothe I saye,
 Ay span seemed thaem to bee;
Handes brade, vytouten nay,
 And fingeres lange, he sheued me.

 Both the ballad and the medieval narrative give four lines to the episode of the throwing of the stone (Herd 3, *AYY* 4b);

He took up a meikle Stane
  And he flang 't as far as I could see;
Tho I had been a Wallace wight
  I couldna liften 't to my knee.

Ay stan he toke op thare it lay,
  And castid forth that I mothe see;
Ay merke-soote of large way
  Bifor me strides he castid three.

The next stanza of the ballad, however, corresponds to two and a half stanzas in *Als Y Yod* (Herd 4, *AYY* 6-8a):

24

O wee wee man
          but thou be strong,
  O tell me whare thy dwelling be;

My dwelling down at yon bonny Bower
  O will you go with me and see.

Til him I sayde ful sone on ane,
  For forthirmare I wald him fraine,
Glalli wild I wit thi name,
  And I wist wat me mouthe gaine;
Thou ert so litel of flesse and bane,
  And so mikel of mithe and mayne;
Ware vones thou, litel man, at hame?
  Wit of the I walde ful faine.

'Thoth I be litel and lith,
  Am y nothe wytouten wane;
Fferli frained thou wat I hith,
  Yat thou salt noth with my name.
My wonige stede ful wel es dyth,
  Nou sone thou salt se at hame.'
Til him I sayde, For Godes mith,
  Lat me forth myn erand gane.

'The thar noth of thin errand lette,
  Thouth thou come ay stonde wit me;
Forthere salt thou noth bisette
  Bi miles twa noythere bi three.'

It seems as though the twenty lines of the longer piece could be a mere inflation of a four-line stanza like that in the ballad, for the extra material does not further the action but merely marks time. The narrator asks what the little man's name is but he will not tell it (6a, 7a); the narrator pleads to be allowed to go on his way but is overborne (last two lines of 7, 8a). Even within 6b, which is close to the ballad, there is, it seems to me, a suggestion of inflation in the otiose final line, 'Wit of the I walde ful faine'

In group 1 texts, the second half of the ballad normally recounts a journey on horseback in two stages (Herd 5a, 7a):

On we lap and awa we rade
  Till we came to yon bonny Green;...

          *   *   *

On we lap and awa we rade
  Till we cam to yon bonny ha' ...

There is no ride on horseback in *Als Y Yod* and per-haps where it occurs in *The Wee Wee Man* its pres-ence is to be accounted for as a rationalisation of the supernaturally swift journey. *Als Y Yod* has only a single unbroken journey, and probably the second journey in the ballad should be seen as a repetition of the type found in oral compositions

25

or arising in works that are orally transmitted. The reduplication occurs at its most extreme in a further eighteenth-century text belonging to group 1, a slip-song called *A New Scotch Song* in Cambridge University Library (Madden 1255), which has nine stanzas instead of the usual eight. This variant repeats not only the lines on the journey but also the question and answer preceding them (4-5a, 7-8a):

You vee vee Man your dwelling Place,
    Your dwelling Place pray tell to me,
My dwelling is upon younders Green,
    Wilt thou gang along with me and see.

Then up they got and away the Rode,
    Untill they came to the bonny Green,...

    *   *   *

You vee vee Man your dwelling Place,
    Your dwelling Place pray tell to me,
My dwelling is at yonders bonny Hall,
    Wilt thou gang along with me and see.

Then up they got and away they Rode,
    Untill they came to the bonny Hall,...

In the St Clair MS text, representing group 2, there is only a single journey and arrival, as in *Als Y Yod*. The second half of the ballad in this variant runs (5-8):

Up we gat & awa we sped
    Untill we came to yon bonny Dean
And there we lighted & looked frae us
    And there we spied a Dainty Dame

Wi' four & twenty waiting on her
    And they were a clad up in green
Had he been the King o' fair Scotland
    The warst o' them might a been his Queen.

The Castle was o the good Red Gold
    The Cieling o the Crestal clear

26

The board was spread frae east to Wast
And there was fouth o' sonsy chear

The Pipers play'd on ilka Wa'
The Ladys Danced on ilka stair
And e'er ye cd a' said what's that
House & man was a' away

The ending of the introductory section of *Als Y
Yod* which corresponds to these stanzas is as
follows (8b-9):

Na linger durste I for him lette,
    But forth ij fundid wyt that free;
Stintid vs broke no becke;
    Ferlicke me thouth hu so mouth bee.

He vent forth, als ij you say,
    In at ay yate, ij understande;
Intil ay yate, wundouten nay;
    It to se thouth me nouth lange.
The bankers on the binkes lay,
    And fair lordes sette ij fonde;
In ilka ay hirn ij herd ay lay,
    And levedys south meloude sange.

The lady with her beautiful attendants and the
castle made of gold in stanzas 5-7 of the ballad
text are not present in *Als Y Yod* and there is a
possibility that they were introduced into the
narrative at a later date. The four and twenty
ladies, particularly, are familiar in other
ballads (*e.g. Child Waters*, No.63 A.18-23) and may
have been drawn in from them. The final ballad
stanza, however, with its reference to music, has
a fairly direct equivalent in the *Als Y Yod* narrative:

The Pipers play'd on ilka Wa'   In ilka hirn ij herd ay lay
    The Ladys Danced on ilka stair   And levedys south meloude sange.
And e'er ye cd a' said what's that
    House & man was a' away

27

This comparison brings out the likelihood that it is the medieval narrative rather than the ballad that is incomplete. *Als Y Yod* does not progress from this point but abruptly takes a new tack in its next stanza which begins with an address to the audience, 'Lithe, bothe yonge and alde'. If the *Als Y Yod* introductory narrative was indeed based on a briefer work, it seems likely that this source, like the ballad, included the vanishing of the supernatural dwelling that the mortal had been allowed to glimpse.

Inevitably the question of *Als Y Yod on ay Mounday* has to be considered along with that of *Thomas of Erceldoune* which shares the unusual structure of supernatural narrative plus prophecy and also has a ballad counterpart, *Thomas Rymer* (Child No.37).[9] I suggest that in both cases there was a medieval Scottish song (*chanson d'aventure* or ballad) which lived on into the modern period, and that this medieval song was absorbed into a longer English prophetic work intended for recitation. While there is in both cases English manuscript evidence from the medieval period and English printed evidence from the seventeenth[10] or eighteenth century, there would be no trace at all of either of these songs in Scotland but for the records derived from oral sources.

3. HISTORY AND HARLAW

David Buchan

IN THE INTRODUCTION to the ballad numbered 163 in
his collection, Francis James Child wrote, 'A
ballad taken down some four hundred years after
the event will be apt to retain very little of
sober history.'[1] And with this view most critics
have concurred. In fact, it has even hardened into
an axiom and on occasion has produced the para-
doxical situation where ballads which are untrust-
worthy as history are reckoned, *ipso facto*, trust-
worthy as ballads, and ballads which are trust-
worthy as history are looked at askance as probable fabrications. At any rate, that statement of
Child's expresses our general attitude toward the
historical ballads: they are not to be taken
seriously as history. A consideration of one particular historical ballad would suggest, however,
that a too easy acceptance of such an attitude
would be rather rash. The ballad in question is
'The Battle of Harlaw', which is dismissed by
Child as a 'comparatively recent' production, a
view which has become standard among subsequent
editors and critics.

As the *A*-text of this ballad, Child prints what
amounts to one version, which originated from
Charles Elphinstone Dalrymple of Kinaldie; this
version would have been recorded just before 1840.
As his *B*-text he prints the three stanzas in the
1823 *Thistle of Scotland*, which was compiled by
the Aberdeen printer and chapman, Alexander Laing.
Child's rather meagre haul was expanded greatly
when Gavin Greig's collection was published, for
it includes no fewer than nine more versions, all,
like the previous, from Aberdeenshire. The editor
of the Greig collection, Alexander Keith, re-
inforces the Child viewpoint: 'Amid all the variations in the already printed versions and in our

records, there is a distinct and unusual corre-
spondence of stanza with stanza, whereas long
tradition should have left more and greater
changes in so many versions.' The ballad of the
Battle of Harlaw, says Keith, is 'largely unhistorical'.[2]

The battle itself was fought in Aberdeenshire
in 1411, and in its way was a battle of no little
importance. An older generation of Scottish historians used to see it as a battle for the domin-
ation of Scotland, the battle which determined
once and for all whether Lowland Scotland was to
be predominantly Celtic or predominantly Anglo-
Saxon, but this opinion has been modified by
modern historians. They are inclined to see it in
more medieval terms as the result of a feudal
squabble over land, specifically, the Earldom of
Ross. The major claimant for this earldom was
Donald, Lord of the Isles, who, fearing the rapacity of the then Regent of Scotland, the Duke of
Albany, collected a large army of Highlanders and
set out to occupy the earldom's lands in the
Northeast. The people who had most to lose from
this incursion were the burgesses of Aberdeen who,
fearing the rapacity of Donald and his caterans,
helped organise a large body of Lowlanders under
the leadership of Alexander Stewart, Earl of Mar,
to protect the Northeast. The provenance of the
troops, and the edict, customary after a battle of
national importance, that the heir of any man
killed at Harlaw was to receive his ward, relief,
and marriage free from the king, would seem to
suggest that the struggle, if not for the domina-
tion of Scotland, was viewed by contemporary Lowlanders as a more than local defence of Lowland
Saxon prosperity against the onslaught of Highland
barbarism. The battle, later known as 'Red Harlaw',
was bloody and lasted an entire day with, at the
end of it, no apparant result. The next morning,
however, the Highlanders were nowhere to be seen,

30

so victory lay technically with the Lowlanders.[3]
Child's objections to the historicity of the
ballad rest on three major counts. Firstly, there
are stanzas 15 and 16:

Brave Forbës drew his men aside,
   Said, Tak your rest a while,
Until I to Drumminnor send,
   To fess my coat o mail.

The servan he did ride,
   An his horse it did na fail,
For in twa hours an a quarter
   He brocht the coat o mail.

These, says Child, 'have a dash of the unheroic
and...may fairly be regarded as wanton depra-
vations.' Secondly, there are stanzas 21 and 22,
which, contrary to the known facts, describe the
Highlanders as being routed:

An whan they saw that he was deid,[Macdonell]
   They turnd an ran awa,
   ....

They rade, they ran, and some did gang,
   They were o sma record;
But Forbës an his merry men,
   They slew them a' the road.

The next stanza, with disconcerting inconsistency,
says what does accord with the known facts, that
'at gloamin, / Ye'd scarce kent wha had wan.' And
thirdly, there is the prominence of the Forbeses.
Child comments:

The ignoring of so marked a personage as Mar and
other men of high local distinction that fell in
the battle in favor of the Forbeses, who, although already of consequence in Aberdeenshire,
are not recorded to have taken any part in the
fight, is perhaps more than might have been
looked for, and must dispose us to believe that

31

this particular ballad had its rise in comparatively recent times.

Any consideration of the battle, and consequently
of the ballad, is complicated by the dearth of
relevant records, but the foremost historian of
the Northeast of Scotland, Dr.Douglas Simpson, has,
on the basis of the material available, reconstructed the campaign and the battle in his book
The Earldom of Mar. This reconstruction sheds much
light on the problems raised by Child. To take the
last objection first: Dr.Simpson points out that
the Forbeses were the Earl of Mar's most powerful
vassals in the Northeast, and that, given the
nature of feudal obligations, it would be inconceivable that they would not play a significant
part in the campaign. This belief is reinforced by
a long-standing family tradition among the Aberdeenshire Forbeses that they rendered signal ser-
vice to Mar on this occasion.[4] It can be safely
assumed that the Forbeses took part in the battle.
What then of the other two objections? How do we
account for the leader of the Lowlanders breaking
off the fighting to send to Drumminor, the head
seat of the Forbeses, for a coat of mail that
takes two hours in the coming, but on arrival
makes the crucial difference between defeat and
victory?

Dr.Simpson indicates that though Mar knew
Donald's destination, the burgh of Aberdeen, he
would not know Donald's approach route, whether he
would come through the Garioch or through the
Rhynie Gap into the Glen of Brux. As Mar could not
cover both approaches by falling back on the city
without leaving the Lowlands open to the ravages
of the caterans, he would have to try to block
both the approach routes at the points where the
Highlanders would debouch on the Lowlands. He
stationed himself, as we know, at Harlaw, to block
the first route. The second route, through the
Rhynie Gap, would bring Donald out at the lands of

Brux, and these lands belonged to the Forbeses. So the obvious thing for Mar to do would be to leave his strongest vassals on their own lands to block this second route. When Mar realised that Donald had chosen the first route he would have to send a messenger to the Forbeses to bring them hotfoot to Harlaw. They would, of course, arrive late, but ready for the second stage of the battle, and could claim, like Blucher a few hundred years later, that their extra numbers had made the decisive difference in the outcome of the battle. This interpretation would explain why the ballad account of the battle falls into two stages, and why the sending to Drumminor had such a crucial effect on the way the battle went. It would also dissolve the remaining objection of Child by explaining away the apparent incongruity of stanzas 21, 22, and 23. The ballad was obviously composed from a Forbes viewpoint, that is, it deals largely with the part played by one section of the Lowland army. If this section arrived at the battlefield with the advantage of surprise and comparative freshness it would probably have the upper hand over the wearied wing of the enemy that it attacked. This, at Harlaw, would give us stanzas 21 and 22, in which the Forbeses rout their immediate opponents. This victory on one wing would satisfactorily relieve the pressure on the rest of the army, but, as the rest of the army was in dire straits, it would not automatically produce a large-scale victory. What we have, in effect, in stanzas 21 and 22, and then 23, are two camera shots: the close-up of the Forbes victory on one wing and the long shot of the battle as a whole. Ironically, then, the points which Child adduced as evidence of the ballad's youth are in fact the points which would indicate that the ballad reflects with a fair degree of accuracy the actual pattern of events, as far as we can ascertain what that pattern was, in the battle itself.

Though Child's objections are the major ones, other details in the ballad have evoked sceptical responses. The sceptic would say that the entire first scene is quite out of tone with the rest of the ballad. Instead of preparing us for a cataclysmic encounter, it concentrates on burlesquing a Highlander's attempt to speak Scots, an effect reinforced by the refrain which imitates the skirl and drone of the pipes. Again, the sceptic can point to the fact that the opponents of the Highlanders are referred to at some place in most of the records as 'redcoats', an anachronism of a few hundred years, and declare the ballad merely an unhistorical palimpsest. Now if, instead of dismissing the whole thing as a farrago, we accept the basic premise that the ballad does reflect, although sometimes in a Hall of Mirrors fashion, the actual pattern of events in the battle, and look at the unhistoricities in the light of this, there is a chance that we might find out something about the nature of the folk imagination and the ways it operated upon its material.

To understand the nature of the two peculiarities, the burlesquing and the redcoats, one must first consider the relations between the Highlands and the Northeast Lowlands. It is a fact insufficiently recognised outside its borders that Scotland has contained for much of its history two nations, with different social organisations, different customs, different languages, and a mutual distrust. The Northeast was a border region, abutting the Highlands, which naturally brought the folk of the Northeast into contact, mainly warlike but sometimes commercial, with the Highlanders. In the eyes of the Northeasterner, the Highlander was to be feared because of his depredations, but he was also looked upon as a rather comic fellow, wild yet courteous, proud yet naive, whose comic side became very pronounced when he tried to grapple with the foreign tongue of Lowland Scots. The Lowland attitude is eloquently summed up in the Scots word for the John Hielanman stereotype —he is a 'tyeuchter'. This dual view of the Highlander as at once a feared raider and a comic figure runs right through Scottish literature from Dunbar to Fergusson. I need only mention the famous poem from the Bannatyne Manuscript, 'How the First Hielandman was Made by God of ane Horse Turd', with its incisive quatrain:

God turned owre the horse turd with his pykit staff,
And up start a Hielandman black as ony draff.
Quod God to the Hielandman, "Where wilt thou now?"
"I will doun in the Lawland, Lord, and there steal a cow."[5]

This is the attitude that is reflected in the first scene of the ballad, which, while burlesquing John Hielanman, uses a number of repetitive devices to remind us that the Highlanders are 'A-marchin tae Harlaw'. In short, the first scene is, *inter alia*, a correlative for the Lowland folk's emotional attitude to the Highlanders.

What about the redcoats? It would appear that the folk had conflated two incursions of Highlandmen more than three hundred years apart, in 1411 and 1745. Can we, however, just leave it at that? What were the reasons for this conflation? These two incursions were alike in being exceptional; they were no mere forays, but of national as well as regional importance. And yet this explanation is far from being satisfactory. There was one large difference between the two incursions: in 1411 the Northeast was united in arms against the Celts, but in 1745 the Northeast was comparatively passive, watching a struggle between Charles's Highlanders and the Government's redcoats, more than half of whom were Hanoverian mercenaries. The Highlanders were unpopular, but the Government levies were equally disliked. This difference is interestingly reflected in Greig's *A*-text, re-

corded at the beginning of this century. In most
versions of the ballad the opening stanza runs
something like this:

As I cam in by Dunidier,
  An doun by Netherha,
There was fifty thousand Hielanmen
  A-marching to Harlaw.

It is followed by a series of stanzas designed to
give an impressionistic effect of the Hielanmen's
march forward. In Greig's *A*-text, however, the
opening stanza reads:

As I cam in the Geerie lan's,
  An' in by Netherha',
I saw sixty thoosan redcoats
  A' marchin to Harlaw.

and is followed five stanzas.later by:

O yes, me was near them,
  An' me their number saw;
There was ninety thoosan Hielanmen
  A' marchin to Harlaw.

This repetition effectively suggests a disengage-
ment, a watching of two armies. The way in which
this new view of the battle, as a fight between
Highlanders and redcoats rather than Highlanders
and Lowlanders, was infiltrating the old can also be
see in Dalrymple's version. His stanza 11 reads:

The Hielanmen, wi their lang swords,
  They laid on us fu sair,
An they drave back our merry men
  Three acres breadth an mair.

He gives as a variant for the third line, 'An they
drave back our merry men,' 'An they drave back the
redcoats.' Here again, emotional commitment to one
side against the other gives way to objectivity.

  There is a shift in the emotional attitudes
implicit in the ballad. It would seem that a

ballad dealing with the 1411 encounter was in the process of being altered to a ballad dealing with the 1745 encounter. Why should this have happened? After the 1745 rebellion and the breakup of the clan system by the Heritable Jurisdictions Act of 1747, relations between the Northeast and the Highlands altered decisively. The Highlanders were driven by economic necessity to come to social terms with the Lowlanders, and, though it took a considerable time, the old barriers of suspicion and distrust were gradually broken down. In brief, the attitude of the Lowland folk to the Highlanders changed, and the ballad reflects the change in attitude. The earlier event was a suitable correlative for the earlier attitude of the folk to the Highlanders, but unsuitable for the later attitude; the newer event, however, was a suitable correlative for the new, more neutral attitude. The supersession of the one event by the other is not merely gratuitous; it answers the folk's need for different correlatives for different emotional attitudes.[6]

The ballad, then, despite the initial impression it is likely to give, is historical in a rather extraordinary way. It reflects, although in blurred fashion, what is reckoned to be the actual pattern of events in the battle, and this pattern, it is worth remarking, is not recorded in any known document, but only in the ballad. What appears to be the ballad's largest unhistoricity actually reflects the kind of historical truth that normally never finds its way into the documents, the nature and quality of the folk's emotional attitudes over a long span of years. And the ballad's interest is more than just historical, for it also provides us with a fair insight into the ways in which the folk imagination reacted to, moulded, and used for its own emotional purposes, the raw material of historical event.

Child's objections can now be seen in perspective, but there still remains Keith's argument that

if the ballad were really old there would be much
greater variation in the recorded versions. To
solve this problem one must trace a hypothetical
history of the ballad. The ballad was composed
soon after the events of 1411 and must have gained
some acceptance, for in 1549 the *Complaynte of
Scotland* mentions it, and references to the tune
crop up in various places in the seventeenth and
eighteenth centuries. It was first recorded in the
early 1820s by Alexander Laing; and with Laing we
have the key to the problem. Laing made his living
both as printer and as chapman. In his latter
capacity, he travelled round Aberdeenshire selling
pins, ribbons, and chapbooks and prints to the
farm servants, and while on his travels he would
pick up from his customers some of their songs,
which, on his return to Aberdeen, he would print
up, publish, and sell back to his rural clientele;
it was a cycle for everybody's benefit. Laing, we
know, was the first man to collect the ballad. He
would print only three stanzas of this 'burlesque'
in the *Thistle of Scotland* because the book was
for him a prestige publication, a genteel and
scholarly production, but he also, I suggest,
would prosecute his normal practice and hawk the
ballad in printed single-sheets round the farm
servants of Aberdeenshire. The versions of the
ballad which we have, then, are not versions of a
ballad composed near 1411, but versions of the one
record of that 1411 ballad collected by Laing and
disseminated in his usual fashion through Aberdeenshire.

The historical ballad, it would appear, is perhaps more historical than it has been given credit
for. But is 'The Battle of Harlaw' an isolated
case? A brief glance at another Aberdeenshire
ballad, 'Edom o Gordon', would suggest not. After
careful consideration of the historical authorities, Child decided that Towie castle had been the
scene of the event described in the ballad, in

which choice he has been followed by every editor.
Dr Douglas Simpson, however, has shown that the
locale could not have been Towie castle as it
was not built until the seventeenth century,
and that the scene was in fact Corgarff castle.
Scrutiny of the five local versions of the ballad
would lead one to the same locale. Not one of
the five refers to Towie castle. Child *E* has
Cargarff, and Greig *B* and *C* both have Corgraff.
Greig *B* has also a reference to Cragie, while
Child *H*, collected from the Southwest, speaks of
Craigie North. These two words, 'Cragie' and
'Craigie', are probably contracted and metath-
esized renderings of Carriegill, or Corriehoul,
the demesne lands of Corgarff. The confusion has
presumably arisen from misinterpretation of
phrases like the one that occurs in Greig *A* —
'Towie's hoose'. In the Northeast of Scotland it
is still customary in rural districts to refer to
a man by the land he owns or farms rather than by
his surname; after this fashion, Geordie Smith,
the tenant-farmer of Cairnmore, is normally referred to as 'Cairnmore'. The phrase 'Towie's hoose'
does not, therefore, pertain to an actual edifice
named Towie, but simply to the residence of Towie
himself, or, to give him his full due, John Forbes
of Towie. In locating the event at Corgarff, the
Northeast versions of 'Edom o Gordon' are in ac-
cordance with the findings of modern research.
Again it would seem that a historical ballad can
be more accurate historically than we generally
anticipate.[7]

The historical ballads, we would all agree, are
no 'documents', but the evidence just presented
would indicate that they can be much nearer to the
truth than is normally realized. They can contain
factual truths that are not found in the often
scanty records, and they can contain emotional
truths, the attitudes and reactions of the ballad-
singing folk to the world around them. Given the

39

nature of these emotional truths, it might prove
fruitful to investigate historical ballads along
joint aesthetic and sociological lines, since this
ballad has shown how a historical event is made to
serve as an aesthetic correlative, an aesthetic
correlative which fulfils a certain sociological
function in that it focuses the emotional concep-
tions of a particular culture. Given the nature of
the factual truths, the moral in general would
seem to be: 'Gyang cannily, and look closer.' At
any rate, we can no longer hold it as axiomatic
that 'the historical ballads fly in the face of
all history.'

4. *THE GREY SELKIE*

Alan Bruford

'THE GREAT SILKIE of Sule Skerry' (Child 113),
being a supernatural ballad, should 'have followed
No.40 had I known of it earlier'.[1] Not only the
number but the title was unfortunate: other versions speak of the grey, not the great selkie, and
'silkie' with an *i* is a relatively rare form of
the word for a seal which is normally 'selkie' or
'selch(ie)' throughout Scotland, including the
Northern Isles.[2] But the one text known to Child
(hereinafter, 'A') is exceptional in other ways.
Though it may well represent the oldest extant
form as well as being the first collected version
of the ballad, it is also the shortest complete
version and the only one to come from outside
Orkney. It was collected by Lieut.(later Capt.)
F.W.L.Thomas, 'from the dictation of a venerable
lady-udaller, who lived at Snarra Voe, a secluded
district in [Unst,] Shetland', and 'sung to a tune
sufficiently melancholy to express the surprise
and sorrow of the deluded mother of the Phocine
babe'.[3]

                    A

1 An eart'ly nourris sits and sings,
     And aye she sings "Ba lily wean;
  "Little ken I my bairnis father,
     Far less the land that he staps in."

2 Then ane arose at her bed fit,
     An' a grumly guest I'm sure was he;
  "Here am I thy bairnis father,
     Although that I be not comelie."

3 "I am a man upo' the lan',
     An' I am a Silkie in the sea;
  And when I'm far and far frae lan',
     My dwelling is in Sule Skerrie."

4 "It was na weel," quo' the maiden fair,
   "It was na weel, indeed," quo' she;
   "That the Great Silkie of Sule Skerrie,
   S'uld hae come and aught a bairn to me."

5 Now he has ta'en a purse of goud,
   And he has pat it upo' her knee;
   Sayin' "Gie to me, my little young son,
   An' tak thee up thy nourris fee."

6 "An' it sall come to pass on a simmer's day,
   Quhen the sin shines het on evera stane;
   That I will take my little young son,
   An' teach him for to swim the faem."

7 "An' thu sall marry a proud gunner,
   An' a proud gunner I'm sure he'll be;
   An' the very first schot that ere he schoots,
   He'll schoot baith my young son and me."

Child himself notes another fragment, also from
Shetland and apparently independent, sent in to
Karl Blind by his correspondent George Sinclair,
jr., a Shetlander living in New Zealand:[4] we may
call this 'C', since it is not the next version
collected.

C

"I am a man upo' da land;
   I am a selkie i' da sea.
An' whin I'm far fa every strand
   My dwelling is in Shööl Skerry."

Bronson's monumental supplement to Child[5]
quotes only one more text and a tune, which do not
in fact belong together. The tune was collected by
the late Professor Otto Andersson of Åbo, Finland,
on a trip to Orkney in 1938, from Mr (John?) Sinclair, Flotta, once more to the words corresponding to A3: F below seems to be his text, as given
by Andersson:

F

I am a man up-on the land. I am a Sel-chie in the sea. And when I'm far from eve-ry strand, my dwell-ing is in Sol-sker-rie.

A full set of words was added by Andersson on each occasion when he published the ballad.[6] Bronson apparently uses those from the later, English article printed in 1954, which are based on a transcript from *The Orcadian* of 11 January 1934, though his notes suggest that he is using those from the earlier Swedish article printed in 1947. The latter were supplied by Miss Anne G.Gilchrist of the English Folk Dance and Song Society, and the only major difference seems to be that A5 is introduced in place of the ninth verse. I am grateful to my friend Mr Ernest Marwick for pointing out what must be the ultimate source of both these texts in a nineteenth-century travelogue, R.Menzies Fergusson's *Rambling Sketches in the Far North and Orcadian Musings* (London, 1883). D below follows the first edition, but the only substantial difference in the later edition is the use of the more conventional spelling for Sule Skerry.[7]

Fergusson seems to have known the South Isles of Orkney best, judging by his travels and the vocabulary of his own dialect lullaby, 'Ba, ba, lammie noo' (pp.159-60). It was 'a South Isles correspondent' who later sent in the ballad to *The Orcadian*, and it seems likely that it is a South Isles text. Certainly, as the parallel texts below show, it is very like G, a version which I recorded from James Henderson, Burray, a native of

43

Gairth, South Ronaldsay.[8] Mr Henderson learned the ballad from the singing of his mother (born Isabella Dass) before 1918. He tells me that his mother always broke off singing toward the end, and briefly narrated the passage which D also

G

1 There lived a maid in the Norway lands:
    "Hush ba loo lilly," she did sing;
  "I dinna ken where my babe's father is
    Or what lands he travels in."

2 Now it happened one night
    As this fair maid lay fast asleep
  That in there came a grey selkie
    And laid himself down at her bed feet,

3 Crying, "Awake, awake, my (?) pretty maid,
    For thy babe's father's sitting at thy bed
      feet.

4 "For I'm a man upon the land,
    A selkie in the sea,
  And I do come from the Wast'ard o Hoy
    Which wise men do call Sule Skerrie.

5 "My name it is good Hyne Malair:
    I earn my livin by the sea,
  An when I'm far from ev'ry shore
    It's then I am in Sule Skerrie."

6 "Oh what a fate, what a weary fate,
    What a weary fate's been laid for me,
  That a selkie should come from the Wast'ard o
      Hoy
    To the Norway lands to have a babe with me."

7 "Oh I will wed thee with a ring,
    With a ring, my dear, I'll wed with thee."
  "Thou may wed thu's weds[9] with whom thou wilt,
    But I'm sure thou'll ne'er wed none wi me."

44

gives in prose before singing the last verses:
thus, though he has forgotten a few lines or even
verses towards the end, this gap is not the result
of his lapse of memory, and may well have been a
regular feature of the ballad.

D

1 In Norway lands there lived a maid.
   "Hush, ba, loo lillie," this maid began,
   "I know not where my baby's father is,
   Whether by land or sea does he travel in."

2 It happened on a certain day,
   When this fair lady fell fast asleep,
   That in cam' a good grey selchie,
   And set him doon at her bed feet,

3 Saying, "Awak', awak', my pretty maid,
   For oh! how sound as thou dost sleep!
   An' I'll tell thee where thy baby's father is;
   He's sittin' close at thy bed feet."

4 "I pray, come tell to me thy name,
   Oh! tell me where does thy dwelling be?"
   "My name it is good Hein Mailer,
   An' I earn my livin' oot o' the sea.

5 "I am a man upon the land;
   I am a selkie in the sea;
   An' whin I'm far frae every strand,
   My dwellin' is in Shool Skerrie."

6 "Alas! alas! this woeful fate!
   This weary fate that's been laid for me!
   That a man should come frae the Wast o' Hoy,
   To the Norway lands to have a bairn wi' me."

7 "My dear, I'll wed thee with a ring.
   With a ring, my dear, I'll wed wi' thee."
   "Thoo may go wed thee weddens wi' whom thoo
        wilt;
   For I'm sure thoo'll never wed none wi' me."

45

8 "Then thou shalt nurse thy little wee son
   For seven long years upon thy knee:
   And at the end of seven years
   I'll come an pay thy nurse's fee."

9 It's oh, she's nursed her little wee son
   For seven years upon her knee:
   And he's come back a gay gentleman
   With a coffer[10] of gold and white monie.

10 She says, "I'll wed thee with a ring,
   With a ring, my dear, I'll wed with thee."
   "Thou may wed thee's weds[9] with whom thou wilt,
   I'm sure thou'll ne'er wed none wi me.

11 "But you will get a gunner good,
   And aye a good gunner he'll be,
   And he'll gaeng out on a Mey morning
   And he'll shoot the son and the Grey Selkie."

   (So he took the son away, and...)
12   "...I'll put a gold chain about his neck,[11]
   That if ever he comes to the Norway lands,
   It's oh, well knowèd he may be."

13 And oh, she got a gunner good,
   And aye a good gunner was he,
   And he gaed out one May morning
   An he shot the son and the Grey Selkie.

   (Then he returned and showed her this wonderful thing that he'd found, the gold chain on
   the selkie's neck...[11])

14   "...you've done...
   For you have shot good Hyne Malair
   And oh, he was right kind to me."

15 She gied a sigh, sobbed aince or twice,
   And then her tender hert did brak in three.

8 "Thoo will nurse my little wee son
    For seven long years upo' thy knee,
  An' at the end o' seven long years
    I'll come back an' pay the norish (nursing)
      fee."

9 She's nursed her little wee son
    For seven long years upo' her knee,
  An' at the end o' seven long years
    He cam' back wi' gold and white monie.

10 She says, "My dear, I'll wed thee wi' a ring,
    Wi' a ring, my dear, I'll wed wi' thee."
  "Thoo may go wed thee weddens wi' whom thoo will;
    For I'm sure thoo'll never wed none wi' me.

12 "An' thoo will get a gunner good,
    An' a gey good gunner it will be,
  An' he'll gae oot on a May mornin'
    An' shoot the son an' the grey selchie.

11 "But I'll put a gold chain around his neck,
    An' a gey good gold chain it'll be,
  That if ever he comes to the Norway lands,
    Thoo may hae a gey good guess on hi'."

13 Oh! she has got a gunner good,
    An' a gey good gunner it was he,
  An' he gaed oot on a May mornin',
    An' he shot the son and the grey selchie.

When the gunner returned from his expedition
and shewed the Norway woman the gold chain,
which he had found round the neck of the young
seal, the poor woman, realising that her son
had perished, gives expression to her sorrow
in the last stanza:

14 "Alas! alas! this woeful fate!
    This weary fate that's been laid for me!"
  An' ance or twice she sobbed and sighed,
    An' her tender heart did brak in three.

The ballad, 'known only by some of the older folks' (presumably women, as Fergusson speaks of 'fair Orcadians') in 1883, has survived a little longer than this remark might imply. In fact Mr Henderson remembers it better than many of the other Child ballads his mother sang, partly no doubt because of its Orkney associations, but also perhaps because of its very tightly-knit structure, where each verse leads on to the next logically, and none is superfluous. The language is admittedly more influenced than A by the conventional English of the broadsheet ballads, and forms such as 'thou wilt' appear alongside the Scots 'thou will' in D and have ousted it in G. But there is none of the unnecessary verbiage, in broadsheet manner, which so often mars late northern versions of the older ballads. Much of the ballad is in dialogue, which adds to the dramatic effect. Occasionally a line is repeated without adding anything, but every verse serves a purpose in carrying on the story, which may indeed be analysed in fashionable binary terms:

1 Heroine introduced:
    she laments that she does not know where her baby's father is.
2, 3 Her baby's father appears in seal form, announces himself,
    4, 5 and reveals his name, home and nature.
    6 Heroine reacts, lamenting her fate.
7 He offers to marry her;
    she refuses.
    8 He engages her to nurse his son for seven years.
    9 After seven years he returns (in human form) to pay her (and claim his son.)
10 She offers to marry him;
    he refuses.

48

> G11, D12 He foretells the shooting of him-
> self and his son.
> G12, D11 He (she?[11]) provides a recognition
> token (gold chain).
> 13 The selkie and his son are shot.
> G14 Heroine recognises by the token that they
> are dead,
> D14, G15 laments and dies.

The heroine's refusal to marry her lover and his
refusal to marry her when she later changes her
mind is a common theme of tradition, well known in
broadsheet ballads, but there is no reason to
doubt that it is an integral part of this ballad.
Though A reduces the plot very effectively to a
single scene, preserving the unities of time and
place — the nurse's fee is paid down on the spot,
and the final tragedy is told only in the prophecy — this dramatic device is probably simply
caused by many verses having been forgotten on the
journey from Orkney to Shetland: it is just by
luck that the ballad has been pared to the bone
without the skeleton falling apart entirely. We
may recognise that the language is older than in
the South Isles redaction, but this perhaps means
that we should envisage an early form with the
structure of the latter but the language more like
A.

Mr Henderson has unfortunately never been able
to 'hold a tune', and though he is very willing to
help it has not yet been possible to try to re-
construct his mother's tune by trial and error. It
certainly began on a rising major triad, and was
quite different from the tune below, though
similar in rhythm. This tune is from another South
Ronaldsay man, John George Halcro, whose family
came from Windwick in the South Parish. He learned
it from his father James Halcro,[12] who was a first
cousin to Mrs Isabella Henderson (brother's son
and sister's daughter). Despite the relationship —

perhaps because they lived a few miles apart —
their versions of the ballad seem to have differed
considerably in tune and perhaps in text also.
Unfortunately Mr Halcro has so far been unable to
lay hands on a text which he wrote down in his
father's lifetime, but he has sung me three verses
of a text, which we will call H, equivalent to
verses 1, 4 and 5 of G. The last verse was prompt-
ed by reading Mr Henderson's text.[13]

There remain to be considered two further versions of the ballad, both overlooked by Bronson,

which can be taken as forming a distinct 'North
Isles redaction', though as we shall see some of
the redaction may be conscious and the distinction
is not so great as it appears. Both of them were
collected in the mid-nineteenth century, B in 1860,
E printed in 1894 but gathered together, the collector claimed, over the previous forty years. B
was taken down by Charles R.Thomson, Howar, then
Bailiff or factor of North Ronaldsay, for John
Keillor, the minister of the island. Keillor was
one of several people enlisted by Lady Caroline
Charteris to help her nephew John Francis Campbell
of Islay in collecting traditional material, but
his Orcadian traditions were of little use for the
Popular Tales of the West Highlands, and lay unnoticed among Campbell's MSS in the National
Library of Scotland (MS 50.1.13 f.316) until they
were brought to the attention of David Thomson,
who printed the ballad in *The People of the Sea*
(London 1954, pp.205-7). E is woven into the
extraordinary long poem, 'The Play o' de Lathie
Odivere', which Walter Traill Dennison published
in *The Scottish Antiquary* in 1894.[14] It has been
reprinted in *County Folk-Lore, Vol.III Orkney and
Shetland Islands* compiled by George F.Black (Folklore Society publications 49, 1903) and *An Anthology of Orkney Verse* compiled by Ernest W.
Marwick (Kirkwall, 1949), and has recently been
woven into George Mackay Brown's *An Orkney Tap-
estry* (London, 1969).

It is necessary to dwell a little here on the
nature of this 'play' which seems to be accepted
as genuine, indeed as sixteenth-century, by
Orkney's most considerable living writer, and also
by a prominent Scottish ballad scholar.[15] Dennison's own claim is given in his introduction:

> In the olden times, Orcadians at their convivial
> meetings amused themselves by rude dramatical
> representations, in which lower animals often
> appeared on the scene. In these performances the

51

> menye-singers acted the principal part. They
> were professionals hired to sing, recite or act
> for the entertainment of the company.
> This ballad was at one time represented as
> a drama by the menye-singers.

No other source supports this, and Dennison is our
only authority for the term 'menye-singers', which
looks suspiciously like an attempt to adapt the
medieval German *Minnesänger* to Scots by substitut-
ing an English (not a Norse) first element.[16]
Dennison refers to A as representing 'a few
stanzas of the ballad', so the kinship is admitted.
In fact the traditional core of the 'play' seems
to be the third 'Fit'[17] and the substance of some
verses in the fourth. It is difficult to see the
rest as anything but Dennison's own composition,
occasionally reinforced by lines which can be
recognised as borrowings from other ballads.

At first Dennison's own account seems to claim
only that he was reconstructing from a few fragments, but later it appears that every verse has a
core of tradition:

> It is now well-nigh fifty years since I first
> heard parts of this ballad, and for forty years
> I have been gathering up fragmentary scraps of
> it from many old people in different parts of
> Orkney. But of all my informants, I owe most to
> my late accomplished friend Mrs Hiddleston, a
> lady who, while fully appreciating the beauties
> of modern literature, never forgot the old tales
> and scraps of verse heard in the days of her
> childhood. We were both much puzzled by the
> name 'Milliegare', occurring in a line of her
> oral version. Both of us at length came to the
> conclusion that it was a corruption of Mickle-
> garth, that being the old Norse name of Constan-
> tinople. It is right to say, that while the ut-
> most care has been taken to preserve the orig-
> inal, and to select the best from the versions

recited to me, I have often had to fill in a
word, sometimes a line, in order to make the
sense clear or to complete the stanza.

This is an understatement for the addition of the
better part of eighty extra stanzas, but earlier
nineteenth-century collectors had set no very
good example.

Ernest Marwick, who has spoken to people who
knew Dennison, tells me that by all he has heard,
Dennison was not the sort of man to deceive his
readers in such an elaborate way. He suggests that
the Odivere ballad, if not purely traditional, may
be the composition of some poetic laird of the
seventeenth or eighteenth century which passed
into oral tradition. But such a writer would hardly have used dialect, and an English or Scots
original would be unlikely to have accumulated so
much dialect *vocabulary* as the 'play' shows in a
century or two of oral transmission. Moreover we
have at least one other instance of a deliberately
misleading introduction by Dennison. Of 'The Finfolk's Foy Sang' he writes:

> Among my juvenile papers I found a copy of the
> Finfolk's foy song; but as, when a boy, I added
> some lines to the oral original, and as I now,
> at a distance of nearly half a century, cannot
> distinguish between my tinkering and the orig-
> inal lines, it would be unfair to present the
> lines as a genuine product of tradition... It is
> the only instance of continuous rhymes I have
> met with among our rude native verses, and is,
> so far as I know, a form of verse only used by
> some of the troubadours.[18]

A later note elaborates the fiction: 'I believe
this same Foy Sang is part of an oral drama called
"The Finfolk's Play", once acted by the menye-
singers.' Apart from the lack of a division into
verses and the 'continuous rhymes'— all 35 lines

rhyme on long -a — the only subject-matter is a quite untraditional example of the pastoral fallacy, put into the mouth of the seal-men with their underwater kingdom as its Arcadia. In genuine tradition these beings were considered, like the fairies, to have fallen with Lucifer[19] and were regarded as being at the least dangerous if not actually evil: no traditional singer would dream of putting himself in their place to compose a song beginning 'O' blithe is de land dat's fae man far awa!' and there is no question that the whole poem is Dennison's own. The note with its mention of menye-singers and plays shows the beginning of the process that produced 'Odivere', and the poem foreshadows the favourable view of the seal-people which is also taken in the 'play', where the heroine, though condemned to be burned for adultery with the selkie, is finally rescued by him, and the son is the only one to die — an ending unlike any version of the genuine ballad.

Supporters of 'Odivere' will no doubt consider the strong dialect in many lines as one of its genuine features. But other versions of our ballad are written in pure mainland Scots with hardly a dialect word, in the case of A and B, strongly influenced by broadsheet English in D and G. In fact the lines of 'Odivere' which contain dialect words rather than dialect spellings are hardly

E

1 I heard a lathie ba'an her bairn;
    An' aye shü rockit, an' aye shü sang,
  An' teuk sae hard apo' de verse,
    Till de hert within her bothie rang.

2 "Ba loo, ba loo, me bonnie bairn,
    Ba lo lillie, ba loo lay,
  Sleep do, me peerie bonnie budo!
    Doo little kens dee mither's wae.

ever those which derive from our original ballad
or can be recognised as borrowings from other
Scots ballads, but are largely designed to display
Dennison's dialect vocabulary.[20]

Allowing at least that the sources of 'Odivere'
are dubious, or as Dennison spells it in dialect
'jubish', we may treat its core, the Third Fit, as
largely genuine. In the parallel texts below, this
(E) is given beside the North Ronaldsay text, B,
with which many verses correspond. Where B has no
parallel I have added comments to suggest whether
Dennison's lines are traditional, new composition
or a rewriting of the traditional original. It may
well be that Dennison knew versions of our ballad
from 'different parts of Orkney': the first line
of the First Fit, 'In Norawa a lathie bed' [bade],
is virtually the first line of D put into dialect,
and it is possible that the offer of marriage in
verse 22 below — quite inappropriate in Dennison's
form of the tale, where the heroine is already
married[21] — has crept in from a version of the
South Isles redaction, which might indeed be the
printed text D. Basically, however, it may fairly
be assumed that he was using a version or versions
from his native isle of Sanday, which could be
expected to resemble one from the neighbouring
isle of North Ronaldsay.

B

1 I heard a Mither ba'ing her Bairn
   An ay she rockit an she sang
  She took sae hard upo' the verse
   Till the heart within her body rang

2 O' row cradle an go cradle
   An ay sleep thou my Bairn within
  O' little ken I my Bairns Faither
   Or yet the land that he liggs in

55

3 "Aloor! I dinno ken dee faither,
    Aloor, aloor! me waefu' sin!
  I dinno ken me bairn's faither,
    Nor yet de land dat he lives in.

4 "Aloor! aloor! ca'd sall I be
    A wicked woman bae a' men,
  Dat I, a married wife, soud hae
    A bairn tae him I dünno ken."

5 Dan ap an' spak a grimly gest,
    Dat stüd sae lech at her bed feet,
  "O here am I, dee bairn's faither,
    Alto I'm no' dee husband sweet."

6 "Me bairn's faither I ken do are,
    Na luve sae sweet I'll ever hae;
  An' yet I hae a gude, gude man,
    Dats far awa fae me dis day."

7 "I care no for dee wadded carl,
    I wus his face I'll never see,
  Bit whin sax munt is come an' gaen,
    I'll come an' pay de noris fee.

8 "Hids no' be said doo tint bae me,
    A bodle wirt o' warly gare,
  Sae whin I come, doos get dee fee
    An' I me bairn tae be me heir."

9 "Noo, for de luve I bür tae dee,
    A luve dats brought me muckle sheem,
  O tell me whar dee heem may be,
    An' tell me true dee vera neem?"

10 "San Imravoe hid is me neem;
    I gong on land; an' sweem on sea;
  Amang de ranks o' selkie folk
    I am a yarl o' hich degree.

11 "I am a man apo' de land,
    I am a selkie i' de sea;
  Me heem it is de Soola-Skerry,
    An' a' dats dare is under me.

56

[E 2 c, d and 3 a, b, are doubtful — the lady protests too much, no doubt because here she is married, and Dennison uses two of his favourite dialect words.[22]]

[Certainly spurious — emphasising the adultery element.]

  3 O up than spake a Grimly Ghost
     An aye sae laigh at her Beds feet
  O here am I, thy bairns faither
     Although I'm nae thy luve sae sweet

[Spurious — indeed contradicting the genuine lines of E 3: note that E like B probably had "luve sae sweet" in the preceding verse, as it is echoed here.]

  5 An foster weel my young young Son
     An' for a Twalmont an a day
  An' when the twalmont's fairly done
     I'll come an pay the nourice's fee.

[Very doubtful — again unnecessarily explicit, perhaps to make up for the omission of the "foster weel..." couplet in the preceding verse.]

[The second line is still harping on her shame and must be spurious, but the question, if not its wording, may be genuine: *cf*.D 4a, b.]

  4 Jo Immrannoe it is my name
     Jo Immranoe they do ca me
  An my lands they lie Baith braid an wide
     Amang the rocks o' Sule Skerry

[Not in B but, except the last line, certainly genuine by other parallels.]

12 "Mair or a thoosan selkie folk,
     Tae me a willan sarvice gae;
     An' I am king o' a' de folk,
     An' la' tae dem is what I say."

13 "Oh who can doo de bairn tak,
     An who can doo de bairn save?
     I' dee cald heem doo'l only mak
     De grimby sea me bairn's grave.

14 "Me peerie bairn I'll safely ferry,
     To I hae nather ship or skift,
     Wi' muckle care tae Soolis-Skerry,
     Afore de sin's hich i' de lift.

15 "Bit who sall I me young son ken,—
     An' who sall I me bairn know?"
     "O' a' de selkies i' Soolis-Skerry
     He's be de middlemist o' dem a'.

16 "His megs sall a' be black as seut,
     His croopan white as driven snaw,
     An' I beside him, like the sam'
     I wus tae dee i' times awa'."

At this point we have the clearest evidence of all
that Dennison has been tampering with the text:
the gunner (married by the heroine in A, 'got' —
which may well mean the same thing — by her in D

17 "Me ain gudeman a warrior prood,
     An' aye a stival nave his he;
     An' he may prick or club me bairn,
     When he's a selkie i' de sea."

18 "I fear no dat, I fear bit dis,
     Dat cockra comes an' fiands me here;
     Bit come what may, I come agen,
     An' fetch me bairn i' ae half year.

[No other version makes him king of the
selkies, and I think this, like the prepara-
tory lines at the end of the two preceding
verses, is Dennison's addition.]

[Read "hoo can doo dee bairn tak." Doubtful;
no parallels and the rhyme of first and third
lines is perhaps unlikely.]

[To = "though". The rhyme of "ferry" and
"Skerry" certainly sounds too good to be true.]

  6 But how shall I my young Son ken
     An how shall I my young Son knaw
   Mang a' the Selkies i' Sule Skerry
   He will be midmost amang them a'

[Doubtful — could be added simply as an excuse
to use the words "megs" (fore flippers) and
"croopan" (trunk, body).]

and G, already married to her in B as in E) is too
modern, and all mention of gunners and shooting is
carefully deleted to suit the medieval setting,
and replaced by a stout-fisted warrior with a club:

  7 My husband is a proud Gunner
     An aye a proud gunner is he
   An the first Shot that he will fire
   Will be at my young Son an' thee

  8 I fear nae livin proud Gunner
     I fear nae Mortal man quo he
   For pouther winna burn i saut
   Sae I an thy young Son'l gae free

[Doubtful — perhaps reconstructed on the basis of
a verse like B 8, using a genuine second line from
another ballad?]

19 "For dan he'll be a seeveneth stream,
   An' dan a man agen I'll be,
   An' tak me bonnie peerie bairn
   A' tae de boons o' Soolis-Skerrie."

20 Whin de sax munts were come an' geen,
   He cam' tae pay de noris fee;
   The tane o' his hands wus fu' o' gowd
   De tither fu' o' white monie.

21 De lathie's taen a gowden chain,
   Her wadin boon fae Odivere,
   Shü tied hid roon her bairn's hars,
   Hid for her sake shü bade him wear.

22 "I'm come tae fetch me bairn awa;
   Fare weel, for doo'r anithers wife."
   "I wad dee wi' a gowden ring,
   An' bide beside dee a' me life."

23 "Doo wad no', whin I wad gude wife;
   I winno, whin doo'r willan noo,
   Dat day doo tint doo'l never fiand;
   He's late, he's ower late tae rue."

24 De lathie lived a lanely life,
   An' aften looks apo de sea,
   Still lipenan her first luve tae fiand,
   Bit jubish dat can never be.

At this stage the two versions of the ballad depart so radically from each other that there is no
longer any point in giving parallel texts. Dennison brings home the heroine's husband Sir Odivere
from the Crusades in his Fourth Fit to play the
gunner's part: he and his men set out to hunt
otters, but a selkie runs out of a geo and is
killed by Odivere 'wi' a mester blow'.[24]

Den oot an' spak, een o' his men,
   "Far hae I sailed an' muckle seen,

[I suspect this is inserted to emphasise the belief
mentioned elsewhere by Dennison that seals became
men at every seventh spring-tide.][23]

> 9 O when that weary Twalmont gaed
>   he Cam' to pay the Nourice fee
>   he had ae coffer fu' o' Gowd
>   an anither fu o white money

[Second line presumably editorial, but in
substance this verse, which is essential to the
plot later, must be genuine, whether it derives
from the North Isles version or a South Isles
one.]

[The two inconsistent halves of this verse point
to the use of a different, no doubt South Isles,
version; probably only the third line retains
the original words.]

[Doubtful in wording, but sounds reasonably
authentic because of the use of well-known say-
ings.]

[Bridge passage to next Fit, certainly supplied
by Dennison; such a leisurely tempo of narrative
is alien to the spirit of the traditional ballad.]

> Bit never gowd on selkie's hars,
>   Till noo I see'd wi' baith me een."

Dennison ingeniously adapts a line from the comic
ballad 'Our Goodman' (Child 274) in a form known
in the Northern Isles to serve as his second line.
The selkie is taken to the hall and Odivere calls
on his wife in words adapted from another ballad,
'The Bonnie Hoose o Airlie' (Child 199):

> "Co' doon, co' doon! Lathie Odivare
>   Co' doon, an' see me farly fang...[25]

"Here's de gowd chain ye got fae me,
  Tell me gude wife, whoo cam hid here?"

"Aloor, aloor! me bonnie bairn,
  Me bairn! what am I born tae see?
Me malisen be on de hand
  Dats wroucht dis deed o' blüd on dee!"

With this lamentation, which may be partly based
on tradition, we can leave Dennison's 'play': the
husband and wife flyting which follows and the
lady's eventual rescue by the seals while the men
are distracted by a whale-hunt were certainly
never a part of our ballad.

The ending of B is quite different from all the
other versions of the ballad, though it accords
quite well with the general pattern of supernatural traditions. These selkies, like other
shape-changing beings, here cannot be shot except
with a silver bullet — metaphorically expressed in
B 8 by the phrase 'pouther winna burn i saut'[26] —
so, when the gunner fires, his bullet misses and
hits his wife, who has come to see her son.

  10 Upo' the Skerry is thy young Son
       Upo' the Skerry lieth he
     Sin thou will see thy ain young Son
       Now is the time tae Speak wi he

  11 The Gunner lay ahind a rock
       ahind a Tangie rock lay he
     an' the Very first Shot the gunner loot
       It Strack his wife aboon the Bree

  12 Jo Immranoe an his young Son
       Wi heavy hearts took tae the Sea
     let a that live on Mortal Yird
       Ne'er Mell wi' Selchies o' the Sea.

Though there is little doubt that B was taken down
from an oral, probably a sung, version,[27] this
seems a little contrived: the heroine no doubt de-
serves punishment for her relations with a non-

62

human being, but the sympathetic reference to the *selkies'* 'heavy hearts' in the last verse does not ring true. 'The Skerry' would suggest the North Ronaldsay Seal Skerry, which unlike Sule Skerry is well within sight from the main island, to any local hearer, and it seems not unlikely that these last verses and the unparalleled verse 8 were added by some local person to supply the defective version of the ballad which he had heard. Perhaps he used another existing story as the basis of his plot, and at least one surviving line of the lost verses — 'the very first shot the gunner loot': compare A 7c, 'the very first schot that ere he schoots'. Certainly he was working within the tradition, and his work is much more acceptable than Dennison's.[28]

The less doubtful parts of the North Isles versions show, as might be expected, some parallels with A — the 'proud' gunner, the selkie's first appearance as a 'grimly ghaist', and the lack of the opening reference to Norway as the scene; some with the South Isles versions — the coffers of gold and white money, the fostering for a (varying) period; and some individual features — 'the heart within her body rang', the heroine's married status, the selkie's name and his son's 'midmost' place on the skerry. There are evidently three separate families or redactions attested. It could be argued, following Dr David Buchan[29] that these represent the orally-composed improvisations of three different seventeenth- or eighteenth-century singers working on an 'oral-formulaic' basis, deploying a repertoire of stock couplets, lines and phrases within an elastic plot framework: at some point a singer learned off a version, probably of his own composition,[30] by heart and from then on the variation within the various families has been much less. In favour of this are the totally different names of the Selkie in the North and South Isles redactions, and the different relationships between the heroine and the gunner, quite a basic feature of the plot. Against it are verbal correspondences between all three families in such speeches as 'Little ken I where my bairn's father is' or 'I am a man upon the land'. But it could be argued, particularly on the basis of parallels from the telling of folktales, that certain passages, especially formal dialogue, in a ballad story could be established in a fixed form at an early date while the rest of the narration was carried on in the singer's own words. On the other side it might be argued that the North Isles versions show what deliberate tampering can do to change the form of a ballad, in one instance without forcing it out of oral currency. What we can say is that a single act of creation, and that in Scots though in Orkney, therefore probably not much before the beginning of the seventeenth century,[31] lies behind all the versions. Our ballad may have been based on a tale that had been told in Norse, even on a Norse ballad, but as we have it it was launched into and carried down on a Scots stream of tradition.

It may yet be possible to save more tunes, if not more words, to set beside the versions above. I would certainly like to see one of the genuine tunes sung as widely as the modern composition used for text A by many 'folksingers' of the revival, which is attractive enough but for the slow waltz rhythm which is not like anything in traditional Scottish songs. One judgment on the existing texts may be allowable. Traill Dennison's 'Play o de Lathie Odivere' is a brave attempt to write an extended poem — longer, though not very much, than any ballad actually sung in Orkney[32] — in full Orcadian dialect. The South Isles redaction represents the same Scots ballad which was the basis of Dennison's poem, converted, perhaps by the gradual influence of a new taste rather than by any conscious rewriting, into a song in

the anglicised broadsheet manner. Yet however in-
ferior the language the latter provides the more
concise, more dramatic, more expressive and less
sentimental telling of the story. The processes of
oral transmission may absorb vulgarities from
printed sources at times, but they act as a per-
petual filter to clear out the extravagant and unnecessary with time, and achieve a natural balance
and good taste which no conscious imitator of folksong has the detachment to emulate. I would rather
have had the original Sanday ballad in full, with
its tune, than the whole of Dennison's dialect
epic.

5. *THE GREY COCK*: DAWN SONG OR REVENANT BALLAD? [1]

Hugh Shields

MEDIEVAL LITERARY VERSE in English has few traces of any lyric genre corresponding to the *alba* of the troubadours. The theme is no better attested in English-language folk song of the present day. Doubly deficient in this way, medieval insular culture and its descendants have perhaps no need to be ransacked for dawn songs that may never have existed. It could seem reasonable to conclude that those few manifestations of the *'alba'* situation that occur in English narrative or dramatic poetry — in Chaucer and Shakespeare to mention only the best known examples[2] — are aberrant cases that may be attributed to foreign or scholarly influence. Maybe so. Yet the scanty traces of the dawn song which do occur, including those of popular tradition, are not so superficial as to rule out the question: Was this or that poem conceived as a dawn song of some more or less conventional type having a more or less close relationship with the *alba* of medieval Occitanian and French? This question has been asked already of the folk song to be examined here. But modern criticism has forgotten to try and answer it, distracted by the undoubted, if deluding, fascination of a rival theme.

It is true that the ballad called the *'Grey cock'* is the only known folk song in English which has ever taken for its subject a reluctant dawn parting of two lovers who are of flesh and blood. Not that the theme of a secret night visit is rare in English folk song. On the contrary, its variations are abundant and may be novel; in the *Mason's word*, for example, a visiting lover gets his way by exciting a girl's curiosity about a certain secret word used by freemasons in their meetings, a secret well kept even after he succeeds in marry-

67

ing her.[3] But in English the night visit seems to extend to a scene of dawn parting only whenever the girl is about to be abandoned.[4] A sole exception may be the *Grey cock*: a brief narrative of lovers compelled to part earlier than they might have by the crowing of a cock which was to warn them only at daybreak but which, despite a promised reward, crows by the light of the moon.[5] The two verses which describe the promise and the deception are the most stable part of a varied textual tradition: 'nuclear' verses we may call them, illustrated in this notation of a rendition apparently intended as complete, though the text has been abridged, perhaps by the singer.

Sung by Robert Cinnamond, Aghadealgan, County Antrim
Recorded by Sean O Baoill B.B.C., R.P.L. 24835

♩ = 60 - 80. Rubato

'Fly up, my cock, you're my well-feath-ered cock, And don't cr-ow to the cl-ear day; Your red r-o-sy comb will be of the beat-en gold, And your neck of a sil-ver-y gr-ey.

- Fly up, my cock, you're my well-feathered cock,
And don't crow to the clear day;
Your red rosy comb will be of the beaten gold
And your neck of a silvery grey.

Oh, my cock flew up and my cock flew down
And he then crowed one hour too soon;
This young man he arose and hurried on his clothes,
But it was only the light of the moon.

- When will you be back, my dear Jimmy, she said,
For to wed with a gay gold ring?

68

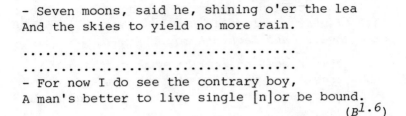

  - Seven moons, said he, shining o'er the lea
  And the skies to yield no more rain.

  ....
  ....
  - For now I do see the contrary boy,
  A man's better to live single [n]or be bound.

              ($B^{1.6}$)

Here is a dawn parting which has parallels in
French songs, both medieval and modern.[6] None of
these, however, has anything like the conclusion
found in a certain number of *Grey cock* versions:
not two flesh-and-blood lovers, but a girl and her
dead sweetheart, or the reverse, are caused to
part by the early crowing of a cock. This supernatural theme casts a quite different light on the
encounter. And we would like to know which theme
was appropriate to the primitive ballad: that of a
forgotten or scarcely practised genre, the dawn
song, or that of the revenant narrative, a familiar topic[7] of British as well as other Germanic
ballad stories.

 Before examining more than twenty variant texts
of the ballad, it will be useful, not to say
necessary, to clear out of the way certain other
songs the text of which has become entangled with
that of our ballad because of thematic analogies.
In doing so we can observe that, if the *Grey cock*
bears a unique thematic resemblance to the *alba*,
yet other songs also contain elements appropriate
to the dawn parting in a variety of contexts.[8] In
the *Drowsy sleeper*, a couple converse 'through a
pane' at the hour when the cock announces daybreak:

 The cocks is crowing, daylight's appearing,
 It's drawing nigh to the break of day.
 Arise, my charmer, out of your slumber,
 Arise, my darling, and come away...[9]

Regret at the approach of dawn is briefly touched

on in an abridged version of a song which I shall
call *'I must away'* (al., *Here's a health unto all
true lovers*, and *Jack the rover*):

> She then arose, she put on some clothing,
> She opened the door and she let him in,
> And into each other's arms they embraced each
>   other,
> Oh, wishing that daylight would have not shine
>   in...[10]

These two night-visit songs usually have one verse
in common, and they could become confused with one
another in tradition.[11] More relevant here are
those casual similarities in each of them that
seem also to have induced textual confusion with
the *Grey cock*.

The *Drowsy sleeper* sometimes ends with a verse
expressing the (unrequited) lover's firm intention
never to return:

> ... - The fish may fly and the seas go dry
> And the rocks may melter down wi' the sun;
> The working men may forget their labour
> Before that I do return again.[12]

Lines corresponding to the first two here are also
spoken by the requited but faithless or dead lover
in versions of the *Grey cock*:

> ... - O when will I see you, my love, she cries,
> And when will I see you again?
> - When the little fishes fly and the seas they
>   do run dry
> And the hard rocks they melt with the sun. (*D*5)

Such expressions of hyperbole are common in traditional poetry. Nevertheless, the thematic similarity of the *Grey cock* and the *Drowsy sleeper*
gives good reason to suppose that one song did
actually borrow the lines in question from the
other. There is no sure proof that they originally
belonged to the *Drowsy sleeper*. Certainly they are

well suited to the lyric character of this song, as well as to the development of its narrative. A girl's refusal to give way, confirmed by her parents' strong objection to the suitor, is more in accord with so emphatic an expression of final parting than is the basic theme of the *Grey cock*: that of shared love marred by a spiteful fowl. But if the textual influence of one song upon the other is conceded, the direction of the borrowing matters little to the relationship which it expresses between our ballad and *one* night-visit song which has nothing supernatural about it.[13]

Textual mingling of the ballad with the other night-visit song, *I must away*, is more easily understood. It occurs in a remarkable amalgam discovered at Birmingham in 1951, where it was sung by a woman who learned it from her father, born in Ireland (E^1). Her song was at once identified as a version of the *Grey cock*, though it actually consists of a bouquet of verses culled from three, perhaps four, different songs including the *Grey cock*. This simple but satisfying conflation has received so much attention that it is especially important for us to recognise its text for what it is.

Verses 1-5 comprise the major part of *I must away*: a song quite often published[14] and possessing a high degree of textual stability that has gone strangely unnoticed (see pp.72-3). British, Irish and Canadian versions of *I must away* show it to be a conventional night-visit song. Some of them refer perfunctorily to cockcrow as a sign for departure, but none gives a special place to the dawn parting. More important, none has a trace of the poignancy that might attend the departure of a lover returned from the dead.[15]

But the Birmingham song passes on from this homely source to a verse in which 'Mary' wonders at the pallor of her visitor and he informs her quite explicitly that he is 'but the ghost of your

continued on p.74

Birmingham song

I must be going, no longer staying,
The burning Thames I have to cross;
Oh, I must be guided without a stumble
Into the arms of my dear lass.

When he came to his true love's window
He knelt down gently on a stone
And it's through a pane he whispered
  slowly
— My dear girl, are you alone?

She rose her head from her down-soft
  pillow,
And snowy were her milk-white breast,
Saying, Who's there, who's there at my
  bedroom window
Disturbing me from my long night's rest?

— Oh I'm your lover, don't discover,
I pray you rise, love, and let me in,
For I am fatigued out of my long night's
  journey;
Besides, I am wet into the skin.

Now this young girl rose and put on her
  clothing
Till she quickly let her own true love
  in;
Oh, they kissed, shook hands and embraced each other
Till that long night was near at an
  end...

I must away: composite text

I must away, I can stay no longer,
The burning tempest I have to cross...
   (o 3 i-ii)[14]
I will be guided without a stumble
Into the arms of you, my dear. (o 2 iii-iv)

When he came to his true love's window
He knelt down gently all on a stone;
It's through a pane, oh, he whispered
   slowly
— My dearest girl, are you alone?

She rose her head off her soft down
   pillow, (o 4 i - 5 i)
Stripping the claes aff her milk white
   breast
Sayand wha's that speaks at my window
Disturbing me o my lang nicht's rest

It's I thy lover do not discover
But rise up quickly and let me in
For I am wearied wi my lang journey
Besids I am wet, love, into the skin
   (c 4 ii - 5 iv)

She then arose, she put on some clothing (h 1 i)
For to let her true love in;
They kissed, shook hands, and embraced
   each other
And then the long night was at an end.
   (b 6 ii-iv)

Willy-O'. The names, first mentioned here, provide
a clue to another source, to be discussed in a few
moments. The next two verses are those generally
stable, and structurally symmetrical, 'nuclear'
verses of the *Grey cock* which describe the trick
played by a domestic fowl. After these comes a
maudlin verse in which 'Willy-O', named again,
urges 'Mary' to weep no more for him. In the final
verse, she asks him when they will meet again and
he replies with the impossibles signifying 'Never'
which have already been quoted.

With the discovery of this text, the problem of
identifying the basic character of our ballad
seemed at first solved in favour of the revenant
hypothesis. Colour was lent to this view by verses
which had had no original supernatural feature but
were retouched in the Birmingham hybrid to suit
the tone of the ghostly Willy and his beloved Mary.
Thus in the second 'nuclear' verse of the *Grey
cock*, the lover goes away '*Not* by the light of the
moon *nor the light of day*', with unwonted stress
upon an eerie, albeit natural, moment of the daily
cycle (italics indicate the retouching). In the
opening verse too, which derived from *I must away*,
his journey had lain across the 'burning Thames'.
One writer claimed that this phrase showed a
'force of belief in the dark spirit world separated from the kingdom of the living by the river
of fire, a painful journey without sun, moon or
star'.[16] Maybe it did for the singer; and it is
true that one Irish version of *I must away* — which
relegates the corresponding line to the conclusion,
'To the burning temples, love, I have to go'[17] —
also evokes, and if anything better, a place of
abode outside this world. Yet every other text of
this song I have consulted speaks only of such
natural obstacles as commonly test the constancy
of lovers in their nocturnal comings and goings:
'hills and mountains', 'those weary mountains',
'the Belfast mountains', 'many the mile', 'the

74

sweet Bann water', 'the storm and tempest', 'this
morning tempest', 'the burning tempest' etc.[18]
And we shall see in a moment why the Irish version referred to differs from these straightforward night-visit texts.

Turning to the Willy-and-Mary verses of the
Birmingham song, we can identify their source
without difficulty. From the mid-nineteenth century dates *Willy-O*, an Anglo-Irish broadside
ballad popular in Irish oral tradition though only
recently reprinted.[19] *Willy-O* is substantially a
rejuvenation of the theme of *Sweet William's ghost*
(Child 77) in deliberate and explicit style; and
vv.6 and 9 of the Birmingham song are pure *Willy-O:*

6 - Willy dear, oh dearest Willy,
    Where is that colour you'd some time ago?
    - Oh, Mary dear, the clay has changed me,
    I am but the ghost of your Willy-O...

9   When she saw her love disappearing
    The tears down her pale cheeks in streams did
        flow;
    He said, Weep no more for me, dear Mary,
    I am no more your Willy-O...

Willy-O[20]

6 - O Willy dear where is the blushes,
    That you had some time ago,
    - O Mary dear the clay has changed them,
    For I am the ghost of your Willy-O...

10 When she saw him disappearing,
    Dow[n] her cheeks the tears did flow,
    - Mary dear, sweetheart and darling,
    Weep no more for your Willy-O.

Furthermore, the single — Irish — version of *I
must away* which casts an unearthly glow upon the
night visit with its return to 'burning temples'
is like the Birmingham text, doing so to conform

75

with the spirit of a supernatural visit. For it
too borrows from *Willy-O* and with the borrowing
introduces names for a couple who have managed up
to that moment very well without them; its pen-
ultimate verse corresponds to the first of those
already quoted:

> Saying, Willy, Willy, where is your flushes?
> Where is your flushes you had years ago?
> Saying, Molly Bawn, sure, cold clay has changed
>   them,
> The raging sea's between me and you...[21]

The composite nature of the Birmingham song is
thus apparent. But the bouquet was culled on more
than one occasion. Most of the verses (1-6, 9)
reproduce a version of *I must away*, presumably
Irish, which had already been augmented by verses
of *Willy-O* and which is at present known only in
the 'burning temples' text. Fresh blooms were
later drawn from the *Grey cock* to introduce the
bird's trick (vv.7, 8, the nuclear verses of the
ballad). With these came the expression of final
parting we have already noted — 'When the fish
they fly etc.'— unless this was a separate and
direct borrowing from the *Drowsy sleeper*, which
seems unlikely.[22]

The textual criticism of orally transmitted
verse is rarely so straightforward. But we have
still to reckon with the chances of thematic recreation of 'the dark spirit-world'. Could Mrs
Costello, the Birmingham singer, have been re-
invigorating an old ballad type in joining the
supernatural, but vulgarly modern, *Willy-O* with
the untimely parting before daybreak which is the
nucleus of the *Grey cock*? One question to ask is:
what could have been the motivation of a return
from the dead linked with this nucleus? We know of
early revenants who have vengeance to wreak, a
complaint to make, a warning to give or a plighted
troth to take back. The Willy of *Willy-O* is not

one of these; like many latter-day revenants he is just dead: a tedious ghost who could at best be a usurper in the *Grey cock*. We must look elsewhere for evidence of supernatural essence in the ballad.

Earlier evidence of an unearthly *Grey cock* narrative can indeed be found. Once again, Ireland figures in the tradition, preserving the oldest text of a version which is quite explicit in its description of a ghostly visit. In the second of this text's three eight-line verses, the cock plays the usual trick. But in the first, the visitor is seen to be a girl and the young man is unaware that she is dead, while in the third she describes what it is like in the grave:

> ... - And where is your bed, my dearest dear? he
> said,
> And where are your white holland sheets?
> And where are the maidens, my dearest love, he
> said,
> That wait on you while you are asleep?
> - The clay is my bed, my dearest dear, she said,
> The shroud is my white holland sheet;
> The worms and the creeping things are my wait-
> ing maids,
> To wait on me whilst I am asleep (D^1)

Various problems of narrative are posed by this version, both in its Irish text and in all other texts noticed, which are without exception Canadian (D^{2-7}). Why is the revenant a girl? Among old ballads, *Fair Margaret and sweet William* (Child 74), and rather more plainly its broadsheet derivative *William and Margaret*[23], present a somewhat analogous situation. Can these have influenced the *Grey cock*, causing the supernatural theme to intrude?[24] Yet the question and answer quoted make little sense during a girl's visit to her lover's house, for why should he ask about her holland sheets and waiting maids as though she should come

77

accompanied by them? Why should she come at all:
even dead, she is unexpected in the visiting
function, essentially a male one. Two Canadian
texts allow for this (D^2, 3),[25] but present an
even worse incongruity: the living Johnny visits
a female 'revenant' in her own home! Discounting
entirely the idea of a visit, may we suppose the
young man to be asking the question at the grave-
side, where it might seem more appropriate? This
would be to suggest a thematic parallel with the
Unquiet grave (Child 78), and in that ballad the
revenant is often a girl. But the parallel has no
other evidence to support it.

In pursuit of a plausible narrative, we turn to
the three other complete Canadian texts (D^{4-6}),
and these describe a male revenant. Here the ghost
will reply in terms that reveal he has been
drowned at sea: but the girl's question still refers to those 'waiting maids', the 'fair maid', or
the 'maiden sweet that used to wait on you', so
that a feature reasonably apt for a female revenant produces an absurd impression when the revenant is male. Obviously these three texts comprise
a variation of the female revenant version arising
out of discontent with its incongruity, influenced
perhaps by other traditional narratives, but fail-
ing to solve the difficulties.

Thus, out of all the supernatural texts, the
Irish one describing the dead girl's visit is,
despite its shortcomings, the most coherent. Its
concluding question and answer, quoted above, have
something of the old ballad style, though it is
difficult to know how they came by it. The opening
lines are in sharp stylistic contrast, and may
well embody editorial retouches:

   - Oh, you're welcome home again, said the young
      man to his love,
  I am waiting for you many a night and day.
 You are tired, you are pale, said this young man

to his dear,
You shall never again go away...

But Joyce, the editor, declared that he learned
the song in Limerick when a boy, which would have
been in the 1840s; whatever his personal contribution, he can hardly be convicted of so thorough-
ly fraudulent a revision as would have been necessary to change the sex of the revenant.[26] A girl
she is and as such inappropriate, for it is time
to state that visiting girls, dead or alive, have
no proper place in any old ballad which uses the
night-visit frame, as the *Grey cock* does. 'Fair
Margaret' (Child 74) does not break the rule: she
comes to put herself between a married couple, and
it is significant that the broadside adaptation of
this ballad, *William and Margaret*, ignores the
fitness of this procedure by showing a girl who
complains at the bedside of an unattached male.[27]
This is the oldest of a modern progeniture of
night-visiting female ghosts. Male or female, it
is interesting to notice that revenants occur with
especial frequency in Anglo-Irish and Irish
ballads from the nineteenth century. Did the
female revenant of the *Grey cock* originate in
nineteenth-century Ireland? Something of a parallel is noticeable in another British ballad, *Tam
Lin* (Child 39), which was adapted to an Anglo-
Irish form with a reversal of the sexes putting
the girl, not the boy, in fairy power.[28] But the
question is to know whether the female revenant
had any supernatural male precursor in the British
tradition of the *Grey cock*, or whether she is
wholly a creature of modern sensibility, like many
other apparitions orally preserved in folk song.

There is little to suggest a supernatural interpretation of the narrative in any text pre-dating
Joyce's Irish one. The ballad had come to the
notice of the literary and fashionable public as
an *'alba'* in the 1770s; already in 1769 David Herd

had published a four-verse text from Scots tradition (B^1). From the previous year also apparently, dates a Scots MS text in which two extra lines follow Herd's first quatrain (B, below). These lines reappear in Herd's second edition of 1776 (B^2), forming part of three extra verses which he must have obtained from a source not previously available to him.[29] Meanwhile, another text went into circulation in England, from 1771 at least, printed commonly under the title *'Saw you my father?'* (B^3). This agreed in substance with the Scots MS text, but added two half quatrains, instead of one, to Herd 1769. I give here the unpublished Scots MS text with these half quatrains in italics, the first of them taken from the English *Saw you my father?*[30]

Falkirk Muir 6 Sep.^{tr} 1768[31]

Saw you my father Saw you my mother or Saw
  you my love John
  [*He told his only dear,*
  That he soon would be here,
But he to another is gone.]
I Saw ne your father I Saw ne your mother but I
  Saw your true love John

Hes met with some delay that hath cause'd him
    to stay
  but hel be here a non

Up Johnie rose & to the door he goes and (he
    deleted) tirl'd
  at ye pin
the Lassie taking tent & to the door she went
  Sae blyth to let him in

flie up flie up[32] my bonny gray Cock & sleep
  till it be day
your kame (it *deleted*) shall be of the burn[i]shd
    gowd
  & your wings of the Silver gray

The Cock he was fase & untrue he was
  & he Crowd an hour oer soon
The Lassie thought it day & she sent her love
    away
  when (*corr.of* &) it was but a blink of ye moon

The italicized lines extend the opening question
and answer to form parallel stanzas, a trait of
style that might seem popular. But the substance
of the extra lines is not as popular in style as
the rest of the text; like the larger interpola-
tions of Herd 1776, it is marred by 'elegance' of
expression. The four texts mentioned comprise a
single version of the ballad, the most influential
version in modern times;[33] but they conceal from
us the exact circumstances of their relationships.
For convenience we may call this version *Saw you
my father?*, though Herd's title was *'The Grey
Cock'*. It enjoyed great vogue, linked with what
seems an un-traditional air on which 'variations
for the harpsichord, or piano forte, German flute,
or violin and violoncello', not to mention the
guitar, were composed.[34] Parodies appeared, and
Burns tells us that 'Every country girl sings *Saw
ye my father?*'.[35] Probably it was composed in the
1760s and was in perfect truth 'a favorite Scotch
song', as the sheet music editions proclaimed;
some Scotticisms have apparently been corrupted in
the English text, and Scots *fase: was* in verse 4
above makes a better internal rhyme than English
false: was.[36]
    That one of the Scotticisms was an internal
rhyme draws attention to the use of this feature
in texts of the *Grey cock*. Early printed texts
often treat the half-lines as full lines (see n.30).
Many of the *alba* texts in particular, though not
only these, use internal rhyme with some consistency; in the 'nuclear' verses, however, internal
rhyme occurs noticeably less. Evidently the well-
known *Saw you my father?* established and popular-

ized this feature as a recurring formal element of
the text, and influenced later oral tradition in
this respect. Its four early texts all use internal rhyme throughout, except in the verse pro-
mising the cock a reward. *Saw you my father?* is a
re-writing, or perhaps an amplification, of some
traditional text which circulated in the earlier
eighteenth century but of which nothing probably
remains reasonably intact except the nuclear
verses of the promise and deception.

The loss of this older text is regrettable.
Was it a form of *alba* or did it describe a return
from the dead? *Saw you my father?* is almost ag-
gressively lacking in internal traits that would
admit any supernatural interpretation. Yet it begins with an exchange of dialogue which parallels
the opening of an undoubted revenant ballad, *Sweet
William's ghost*. Child's *E* text of this ballad
shows the closest similarity:

> As May Margret sat in her bouerie
>   In her bouer all alone,
> At the very parting o midnicht
>   She heard a mournfu moan.
>
> - O is it my father? O is it my mother?
>   Or is it my brother John?
> Or is it Sweet William, my ain true-love,
>   To Scotland new come home?
>
> - It is na your father, it is na your mother,
>   It is na your brother John;
> But it is Sweet William, your ain true-love,
>   To Scotland new come home...[37]

One may suspect a textual borrowing, and Child is
probably right in thinking that the material
passed from *Sweet William's ghost* to *Saw you my
father?*. In the former, a girl needs to identify
her dead lover before conversing with him; in the
latter, an impatient girl is reassured by an un-
identified third party about some vague impediment

to her lover's arrival. Could this awkwardly circumstantial opening have obscured an older supernatural theme? Lacking further documentation, we can only use personal judgment to decide whether the borrowing from *Sweet William's ghost* does betray supernatural essence in the traditional *Grey cock*. But there is little to suggest that it does. Someone plunders a revenant night-visit ballad to enrich another night-visit ballad with textual booty wholly lacking in unearthly features. It is not an immediately obvious way of making involuntary avowal that the receiving ballad originally described a return from the dead, more especially if the plunderer was, as it seems likely, the mundane author-adapter of *Saw you my father?*

So far, the *alba* hypothesis has been reinforced by narrative implausibility in the revenant texts, by the later appearance of these in places remote from any focus of ballad composition, as well as by their smaller number: though in counting texts or versions, oral or written, we must reckon with the influence of *Saw you my father?* in modern times. But there is also older evidence of an *alba* tradition.

In 1685, almost a century before *Saw you my father?* appeared, an *alba* text of the ballad was printed (A^1) which is more popular in style than any eighteenth-century text, and puts the erotic character of the night visit into full relief. Its fourth verse is a textual motif of songs of seduction and desertion, commonplace in modern oral tradition;[38] and the last two lines, for their part, recall textually the quatrain *Westron wynde*, a love lyric preserved in a MS of the early sixteenth century.[39] The 1685 text is worth quoting in full, with the significant variants of subsequent texts of the same version:

I

I Love my Love, she not me,
    Because I am so poor:
But, poor or rich, she hath my heart,
    And shall have evermore.

II

I went unto my true Loves Gate,
    And knocked at the Ring;
So ready was my own, her self,
    To rise, and let me in.

III

I looked in my true Loves face,
    Methought she seem'd but wan;
I took her in mine arms so wide,
    And carry'd her to bed agen.

IV

Where all the fore-part of the night
    Together close we lay,
And all the latter-part of the night
    She slept in mine arms till day.

V

But cursed be that little *Tirry-Cock*[41]
    That crow'd in the morning so soon;
I thought it had been the dawning of
      the day,
    When 'twas but the light of the Moon.

[VI]

Then up I rose, and donn'd my Cloaths,
    And walk'd it over the Plain;
Wishing my self on my true Loves Bed,
    And her in mine arms again.

CANT.*XIII*   (*p.45*)

I

A Micam Amo, non redamet,
　　Inopiœ gratia;
Vtcunq; siet cor habet,
　Etiam in secula.

II   (*p.47*)

Adibam charœ Posticum,
　Pulsatum annulum;
Assurgit ipsa acturum
　Vt intrem clanculum.

III

Inspexi faciem Amantis,
　Vt visam pallidam;
Extensis[40] cœpi brachiis,
　Portare ad lectulam.

IV

Vbi per noctem mediam
　Imus concubitum;
Ac ibi pernoctaveram
　Vsq; ad diluculum.

V

Vœ autem tibi Gallule,
　Prae gallicinio;
Nocti-lucam putabam esse,
　Pro conticinio.

[VI]   (*p.49*)

Indutis ergo vestibus,
　Planum obambulo;
Optans illam amplexibus,
　Ac me in lectulo.

VARIANTS (*1-5*: Appendix, *A* texts *1-5*) I ii had
lately grown poor *3*, was g. p. *4*/iii-iv But alack,
& alas, I gain'd her h., And she lou'd me for e. *2*.
  II i-ii I w. & bought my t.-l. a ring, And k.
aloud at the door *2*, It was under my t. l.'s
window one night, Yo! there die I, hallo so shillo
etc. *5* / iii-iv My t.-l. arose, & put on her
cloaths, She came down and *2*, *cf*. *3-5*.
  III *2*, *5*, *omit*; ii My heart grew light & fain *3*,
My h. g. cold & faint *4* / iii round the middle so
small *3*, *cf*. *4* / iv And kiss'd the dear maid again *3*.
  IV *3 omits*; ii We did both sport & play *4*, *5*,
I did s. & p. *2* / iv I slept in her *2*.
  V She cries to the cock, saying, Thou must not
crow, Until that the day be worn; And thy wings
shall be made of the silvery gray, And thy voice
of the silver horn. *3* / i My love she kept a cock
and a pretty crowing cock *4*, Now my father keeps
a *5* / iii My love she t. 'twas day & she hastened
me away *4*, I t. it had been day when I sent my
love away *5*.
  VI *5 omits*; i-ii The wind it did blow & the
cocks they did crow As I tripped o. the p. *4*,
As homeward I hied o'er yon lofty hill, The w. it
blew high & cold *3* / iii-iv O 'twas very pretty
play, as I do say, But I'd rather have been in my
t. l.'s arms till day *2*, Then I wish'd I were
safe by my t.-l.'s side again, Her fair form once
more to enfold. *3*, So I w. myself back in my t.
l.'s arms And she in her bed a. *4*.
  [VII] *3 (cf. 4, 5) adds*: Oh I'll be as constant
to my true-love, As the dial is to the sun; And
if she will not be the very same to me, She is
far better lost than won.

  We can be sure, from the traditional language
used here, that the erotic theme it expresses is
no concoction of Henry Bold, the seventeenth-
century editor and latinizer, but part and parcel
of the popular tradition from which he drew his

text. So it is strange to find the modern writer who discovered this text trying to make it serve the revenant hypothesis by diagnosing a ghostly element in the 'wan' complexion of the girl (III ii).[42] The epithet is unwonted, but not at all jarring, in the night-visit context. To be 'pale and/or wan' is indeed an attribute of the ballad revenant; but other ballad characters too may be pale or wan at times of tension. These include pregnancy,[43] and one modern song which seems to allude to this with uncommon bluntness, 'Young girls when they are breeding they looks both pale and wan',[44] is actually concerned in the context, not with pregnancy at all, but with simple love-sickness. Among the 'loose and humorous' songs rejected by bishop Percy is one in which a girl weary of lying alone laments 'Can any one tell what I ayle That I looke soe leane, soe wan, soe pale?'.[45] Other examples of erotic pallor in girls may be easily found.[46] In any case, the variants suggest that the line originally referred to the lover, not the girl, as 'fain', which gives a proper rhyme for 'agen'. For the lover to be 'fain' is certainly not a ghostly reaction. Nor in Bold's text could we overlook the absurdity, recalling two Canadian texts of another version $(D^{2,3})$, of a male visitor carrying a girl who is a ghost back to her own bed.

Though not abundant, the records of this version are diverse in date and provenance, suggesting that it enjoyed long and extensive oral currency in Britain (and probably reached the Isle of Man).[47] Rather surprisingly, it omits the first of the two 'nuclear' verses, with its promise of a reward to the cock, and implies in the second verse no especial malevolence in the bird's behaviour.[48] In these discrepancies from what we have so far considered a narrative norm, there is closer conformity, on the other hand, with the corresponding motif of French night-visit ballads, for example:

> Ils ne fur'nt pas deux heur's ensemble
> Que l'alouett' chanta le jour:
> - Chante! chante! belle alouette,
>   Je te maudis,
> Voilà qu' tu chant's le point du jour,
>   Il n'est qu'minuit![49]

Is the parallel of promise and deception then a late development of insular tradition? No doubt the wily birds which converse with Lady Isabel about the Elf-knight's death in some versions of Child 4 and with the murderess of young Hunting in most versions of Child 68 could have furnished models for elaboration which aimed at constituting a dramatic scene from a lyric verse.[50] It is a fact worth remarking that this version of the *Grey cock* regularly uses first-person narrative, and contains lyric commonplaces, already referred to, which are appropriate to such expression. We cannot rule out the possibility that this lyric form, far from being a deviation from ballad narrative and its style, is actually the source of the ballad we call the *Grey cock*.

Whatever its status, the lyric version provides our *alba* hypothesis with important confirmation, not only by its early appearance but in its similarity to night-visit songs in French and its textual links with other erotic songs in English. On the other hand, the deceitful cock, which it neglects, also seems to belong to an old tradition of which we know too little and which, if better known, might well prove the third-person ballad narrative to be more primitive than my preceding paragraph has tended to suggest.[51] A comb of beaten (burnished, beaming, etc.) gold is not promised to any common fowl. The cock is implicitly given the function of a watcher, it is a familiar creature associated with the girl's home or the girl herself. Like the talking birds of

Young Hunting and *Lady Isabel*, its relation with
the girl is close but equivocal. Celtic, and even
Arabic, mythology have been invoked and their
magic birds adduced:[52] it is unnecessary to range
so far when the beauty of Chaucer's 'gentil'
Chantecler[53] so well recalls the rewards promised
to the cock in our ballad. Even more striking is
an anonymous lyric of the fifteenth century, *I
haue a gentil cook*, wholly given up to the description of a similarly beautiful cock which
perches every night 'in myn ladyis chaumbyr'.[54]
Chantecler is a neutral character so far as lovers
and lovers' ghosts are concerned; but the anonymous cock has evident erotic undertones. At the
same time, it is a well-intentioned creature that
has nothing in common, any more than Chantecler
has, with those awful heralds of the dawn that
crow in ballads to warn ghosts to depart.[55] The
'gentil cook' can well be a precursor of our Grey
Cock, and if it is, the narrative of a return from
the dead is scarcely admissible in the primitive
form of the ballad.

Indeed, if we attribute jealousy to the cock,
we approach a comic interpretation. Comic or
serious, it is apparent from medieval parallels
that the deceitful or misleading bird belongs to
early dawn-song tradition.[56] And we could hardly
imagine a better reduction of the courtly *alba*
theme to a simple narrative motif than that which
is provided by the *Grey cock* in the nuclear verses
of the third-person narrative. In its lyric form,
this motif seems to be of French origin, and quite
without relevance to the Other World of ballad
lore.

Why did this medieval courtly influence not
mark English folk poetry more deeply? Perhaps for
the very reason that the *Grey cock* epitomised the
theme so well; and perhaps also because it is not
a theme especially suited to the Anglo-Saxon
temperament. In folk song in English, amorous ad-

ventures are not usually brought to a successful
and at the same time serious conclusion such as
was characteristic of the *alba*. Many night-visit
songs take a comic or even cynical turn (see n.4);
if they turn to tragedy, this is no better suited
to the *alba* theme. The category of revenant lovers
remains as the only one which evokes, like the
alba, a tender scene of dawn parting. And because
of this common feature, the *Grey cock* has become
the object of what seems almost a conspiracy —
not deliberate certainly but none the less in-
sidious — to turn this unique dawn song into something more conventional in Anglo-Saxon tradition:
a ballad of a revenant lover. When did the first
moves in this direction take place? Not certainly
with the wan girl of the 1685 lyric version, and
probably not with the verses borrowed from *Sweet
William's ghost* by the eighteenth-century *Saw you
my father?*. The tendency seems to be a modern one,
probably not pre-dating the nineteenth century.
Popular and scholarly tradition have both been
affected by it; scholars have been less than
critical in accepting almost any stray evidence
that could be taken as a hint of supernatural
elements in the narrative. Among these I would
class the hyperbolic impossibles (*When fishes fly*
etc.) which have been advanced as a very proper
expression of the irrevocable departure of a
visitor from the Other World, though we have seen
that such expressions, and even the same ones, are
quite at home in the conclusion of a night-visit
song that has no room for supernatural elements.[57]
My own conjecture is that a verse of hyperbole was
first added to the *Grey cock* to introduce the
notion of infidelity in the lover ($B^{1.4-6}$ and
$B^{2.4-5}$), after the manner of such night visits as
Trooper and maid (Child 299), and that the hyperbole was later found quite suitable to the supernatural interpretation. Most of the revenant narratives include it (D^{2-7}, E), whereas most *alba*

90

narratives omit it, among them the lyric version attested in 1685 (A, $B^{1}.1-3$, $B^{2}.1-3$, B^{3}, C).[58]

This article has presented, not 'proof', but a great deal of circumstantial evidence, that the *Grey cock* developed from a medieval tradition of love lyric in which motifs of the early medieval dawn song still circulated. The principal of these to be adopted was the watchful, even deceitful, cock, the nucleus of the ballad narrative; also contributory were the more rarely attested allusions to love play (*all the fore part of the night* etc. $A^{1-2, 4-5}$) and expression of the wish that the night should not end:

> I wish, this maid said she, This night would prove to be
> As long as since the world first began.
> $(B^{2.5}$, cf. $B^{2.4}$ and $D^{1-6})$[59]

Such allusions are no less noteworthy for being deliberately blurred or suppressed through editorial censoriousness.[60]

The *alba* hypothesis is supported by many details, and it is also in accord with the broad lines of European cultural development from the thirteenth to the twentieth centuries. In particular, the reactivation of supernatural themes in lyric poetry, attributable to the 'Romantic movement' in its broadest historical context,[61] may be plausibly regarded as the source of a new supernatural interpretation of the narrative nucleus of our ballad. We may agree in this case that the supernatural world is 'not the essence' of balladry,[62] even if doubts are reserved on the general thesis put forward by the author of this observation: namely, that supernatural ballads of some antiquity are less primitive than related early ballads which have no supernatural features. Leaving aside this broader question, we observe supernatural features in the tradition of the *Grey*

91

cock which belong to a younger stratum than those of *Sweet William's ghost*, the *Unquiet grave*, and other ballads in which a return from the dead is essential to the proper development of the narrative. In the *Grey cock*, a revenant is unnecessary, unmotivated, and, I would add, incompatible with the relationship in which the watchful or deceitful bird stands to the lovers.

At the conclusion of this textual study it may be remarked that all the texts which it has embraced, earthly and unearthly, can be regarded as texts of the *same* ballad. Certainly they form a number of more or less distinct families;[63] yet there is among the families enough evidence of casual borrowing of lines or verses — 'dynamic' textual relationships — to suggest that singers have at various times regarded texts not particularly close to one another as variants of the same song.[64] The melodic tradition is less coherent; obvious relationships between individual tunes are the exception, though tunes fairly often coincide in detailed respects.[65] On the other hand, melodic parallels have been remarked upon in versions of other songs whose textual relationships with the *Grey cock* we have had cause to consider.[66] A thoroughgoing study of inter-related night-visit songs, including the *Grey cock*, could usefully embrace comparative examination of their tunes.[67]

The present undertaking has been more limited than this. Within its limits, I hope it has at least produced enough evidence to discourage, in one particular, the idea that modern popular culture has been uniformly dominated by an urge to rationalise, which it has gratified upon the irrationalities only to be expected of ballads in the medieval tradition.

92

6. MISS REBURN'S BALLADS: A NINETEENTH-CENTURY REPERTOIRE FROM IRELAND

Alisoun Gardner-Medwin

WHILE GATHERING TOGETHER material for his great collection Professor Francis James Child of Harvard attempted to obtain ballads handed down by oral tradition. He sent out circulars asking for help in collecting the remains of ballads; one of these circulars received notice in the columns of *The Cultivator and Country Gentleman*, a paper for the farming communities of the United States, on March 3rd 1881. The notice was observed by a lady then living in Iowa who had been born and passed her childhood in County Meath, in Ireland; this was Miss Margaret Reburn. Over the next year she sent Child several letters, containing parts of many ballads of the kind he was looking for, as well as much non-traditional material. Child was not enthusiastic about her contribution. He wrote 'Some of them quite suspicious' on the front of the folder, yet he did publish some of her fragments. In the light of our present knowledge of oral tradition on both sides of the Atlantic, the time seems ripe for a reconsideration of her ballads.

The manuscript, Volume XVIII of the Child MSS in the Harvard College Library (25241.47F*), consists of seven letters and a group of papers containing the ballads. It is not clear which sheet of ballads was sent with each letter; it is clear, however, that in several cases Miss Reburn sent a few lines at first and more later after trying to remember the whole. Child wrote identifying titles on many of the fragments, although he only published a few. For convenience of reference titles used here are Child's and the verse has been divided into stanzas. Miss Reburn used scarcely any punctuation, nor did she divide the verse. For

the sake of clarity I have provided a table of
contents of the manuscript in an Appendix.

Miss Reburn was an enthusiast; she sent Child
everything she thought might be of use. She was
convinced that she was sending material from oral
tradition, as Child had requested in his circular.

> I heard them sometimes in the Sixties [1860's]
> and in the county of Meath but from no person in
> particular they were as popular and as common as
> the Negro Melodies of this country Everyone sung
> them everyone knew fragments of them Those trad-
> itionary Ballads all the modern Scotch songs of
> which we were passionately fond and Moore's
> Melodies constituted our Capital in singing
>
> (Letter 3)

Yet as well as true traditional ballads that show
signs of oral transmission there is much material
that must have come almost directly from print.

Among those of Miss Reburn's ballads that are
close to print one group is noteworthy. Six
ballads, *Earl Walter* (connected with Child 63
Child Waters), *Young Johnstone* (88), *Queen
Eleanor's Confession* (156), *Edom o' Gordon* (178),
Sir James the Rose (213) and *The Water King*, appeared together with many other songs in a series
of pamphlets entitled *Charms of Melody, or Siren
Melody*, printed by J. and J.Carrick at Bachelor's
Walk, Dublin, probably between 1810 and 1820,[1] and
comparison reveals that Miss Reburn's texts
closely resemble those in *Charms of Melody*. The
publishers of this series took their material from
a wide variety of sources; some may have been from
tradition, much was from broadsides and chapbooks,
some from previous collectors, Percy and Herd for
example, and even from the writings of Matthew
'Monk' Lewis. His translation of Herder's German
translation of the Danish ballad *Nøkkens Svig*
(*Danmarks gamle Folkeviser* 39)[2] appeared in *Tales
of Wonder*.[3] This free translation, called *The*

94

Water King, was taken over into *Charms of Melody*[4]
and a muddled but word perfect fragment was in
turn sent to Child by Miss Reburn.

    His courser to the door bound he
      And paced the churchyard
    He bound his courser to the door
    And paced the churchyard three times four
    He stepped o'er benches one and two
    Oh lovely maid I die for you
    He stepped o'er benches two and three
    Oh lovely maiden come with me
    The lovely maiden blushed aside
    Oh would I were the white chief's bride

The first appearance in English of this narrative
poem, based upon a foreign ballad, can be pre-
cisely dated. Miss Reburn's words are so close to
the original as to make it clear that she had
learned them by heart when a girl. However, she
denied taking any of her ballads from print, and
indeed it seems more probable that someone of the
generation before her had learned Lewis's poem by
heart and passed it on to Miss Reburn. It is clear
from this example that she was by no means an oral
traditional singer; she is an excellent example of
a literate person who tries to remember the exact
words she learned in childhood.

The other five ballads in this group are found
not only in *Charms of Melody* but also in other
printed forms and in oral tradition in Scotland
and possibly Ireland (88D) in the early nineteenth
century. Miss Reburn's texts are close to those in
Charms of Melody, yet it is fair to say that these
five ballads may also have circulated in Meath in
chapbook form or even orally. The most interesting
of these ballads is *Edom o' Gordon* (178). Miss
Reburn's text is close to the version published by
Percy[5], to that published by the Foulis brothers
in Glasgow in 1755 (Child D) and to a version in a
chapbook dated 1795[6]. All three of these show a

Scottish dialect, whereas the *Charms of Melody* version is anglicised. Since the compilers of *Charms of Melody* drew much from Percy's *Reliques* it might be assumed that Percy was the source for this one also were it not that both the chapbook of 1795 and *Charms of Melody* give the name of the house as 'Towie', as does Miss Reburn ('Towey house', Item 9). This name occurs in *Edom o' Gordon* in Aberdeenshire[7] and these examples suggest that the name 'Towie' was associated with the ballad long before Greig was collecting.

This last example, *Edom o' Gordon*, is of a ballad disseminated in the latter years of the eighteenth century in chapbooks. This may have been the case also for *Fair Rosamund betrayed to the Queen*, one of the many hack pieces on the relationship between Rosamund and Henry II. The example known to Miss Reburn, which begins

In Woodstock bower, once grew a flower
   Beloved of England's King
The like for scent and sweet content
   Did ne'er in England spring

Fair Rosamond of rose like hue
   Enticing so to love
As caused young Henry's royal heart
   The joys thereof to prove

is related to the ballads mentioned by Child in his first collection[8] and current in chapbooks in the eighteenth century[9]. The second of Miss Reburn's ballads about Fair Rosamund, *Fair Rosamund foretells her fate*, may well also be derived from a chapbook; some of it is written in Scottish dialect which suggests a printed source, since it appears in the spelling as well as in the vocabulary. The style of the verse is direct and swift, better than is usual in chapbook ballads. It is unusual among Fair Rosamund ballads in that she does not know who her lover is, and it is interesting because of the 'planet book' divination.

1 My nose it bleeded three times last night
   And syne at the hour of day
What gars my heart like a cake or [of] lead
   And my true luve but ridden away

2 She got down her Planet book
   And read from one till three
And all that she could see therein was
   Queen Elinor will poison me

3 Now fause, now fause, ye lying planet book
   To gar such wierd for me
Our Lady forefend me frae the deied
   Thy love would hae me dree

4 Again she read her planet book
   And read from three till nine
And the planet page said oure & owre
   Thou art King Henry's concubine

5 Now fause now fause ye planet page
   King Henry assoigns not me
To my ain true luve Lord Hugh of Kent
   Ill be leal till my body sall dee

6 Now flowt not the planet page Fair May
   The Stars they ken weal or bane
And thine ain true luve Lord Hugh of Kent
   And King Henry they baith are ane

The Cruel Stepmother is one of the pieces that
must have horrified Child; 'quite suspicious' as
he wrote on Miss Reburn's manuscript. Child's suspicion would have been all the stronger because he
had made a particular enquiry about a ballad along
these lines in his circular.

Woe worth the day when thou wert born
   My bonnie son to me
Wi ithers to share thy father's gowd
   Braks thy mither's heart for thee
But it must na be and it sall na be

Ive sworn and sall not fail
  Scant fare and stripes for sickly weans
    Ower young to tell the tale

This stanza gives some idea of the language and
style of this poem. The cruel stepmother is speaking; she tells how she loved Lord Ronald, in vain,
but gained him after his first wife's death. The
poem changes to the third person, and relates how
the dead mother returns to look after her children,
who are ill-treated by Lord Ronald's second wife.
The second part is of course a story similar to
that in the Danish ballad *Moderen under Mulde*
(*Danmarks gamle Folkeviser* 89) which was translated by Robert Jamieson and published by Sir
Walter Scott in 1810.[10] However, Miss Reburn's
Cruel Stepmother only resembles Jamieson's translation and the Danish ballad in plot outline. A
dead mother who returns to look after her children
appears on a broadside.[11] The *Cruel Stepmother*
collected by Greig[12] does not resemble this text
of Miss Reburn's. The words of her text are non-
traditional, although they contain some Scottish
words and phrases that might be from tradition. It
seems likely that her *Cruel Mother* was written in
the early nineteenth century, possibly influenced
by the translation in *The Lady of the Lake*.
    The Vanquished King is a long pseudo-heroic
ballad about an event that is supposed to have
happened during the Viking period, while Danish
invaders controlled Ireland. The plot is melo-
dramatic and the poem suggests the influence of
the *Gothick* romance of the early nineteenth century. The two opening stanzas will give an idea of
the style.

1 The vanquished King in fight no more
    The Invader's prowess braves
  And proud o'er Tara's regal walls
    The Ostman standard waves

2 The daughter of the vanquished King
   O'Connor's destined bride
 Her maidens slowly sadly bring
   To grace the conquerer's side

The story appears in Keating's *History of Ireland*[13]
and in William Warner's *Albion's England*.[14]
   One fragment given by Miss Reburn I have been
unable to trace.

 Straight to Paris I will go
   For a bottle of holy w[ater]
 Your mother's face I'll wash with grace
   And all your friends I'll flatter

Of the poems and ballads dealt with so far
those that I have been able to trace seem to be
related to printed texts. Some can be seen to be
connected with texts of the early nineteenth century, several of them from *Charms of Melody*. Where
it has been possible to compare Miss Reburn's
text with a printed one it becomes clear that she
sent Child as much as she could remember of what
she learnt by heart as a girl. Her affirmations
that she learned her songs from oral tradition are
more convincing when we come to consider the rest
of her ballads which are known in oral tradition,
and of which her variants show signs of true traditional style.
   The first of these is not a Child ballad, but
one recognised by Laws as a broadside that entered
tradition.

 The ship it then lay in the Downs
 And was for Virginia bound

Slight though this is, it seems to belong to Laws
M 20, *Betsy is a Beauty Fair*.[15] This broadside
ballad was known to Greig and was quite common in
the United States.
   The second fragment is from a folksong called
Siúil a Rúin (or *Shule Agra*), which is well known
in Britain and America.[16]

I'll dye my petticoats I'll dye them red
And round the world I'll beg my bread
And then my parents will wish me dead
Go dhea tha mavoreen slawn

This is one stanza of the folksong; the Gaelic
fourth line is bruised but still recognisable and
the refrain beginning 'Siúil a Rúin' is missing.
Miss Reburn commented on this song:

When Sir Walter [Scott] visited Ireland Miss
Edgeworth's niece pleased him by singing 'I'll
dye my petticoat'[17]   (Letter 4)

This song is said to have originated in the early
eighteenth century;[18] it may have been translated
from a Gaelic original, or perhaps English words
were put to a Gaelic air and refrain. A lady who
knew it in both English and Gaelic was mentioned
by Lucy Broadwood in her notes to a variant from
Waterford:

Mrs. Clandillon writes that my version 'is the
only way I ever heard *Shule Agra* sung in this
country, and it is the very same as I sing in
Irish. I also know your version of the English
words; in fact almost everyone here does.'[19]

In its many variants on both sides of the Atlantic
this song shows clearly how words no longer understood, the Gaelic refrain, degenerate into nonsense.

We now come to those of Miss Reburn's ballads
which are variants of the ballads published by
Child. Of her contributions six were printed by
him and therefore have long been available to
scholars: *The Cruel Brother*, 11 J; *The Cruel
Mother*, 20 M; *Fair Annie*, 62 G; *Little Musgrave
and Lady Barnard*, 81 N; *The Gay Goshawk*, 96 F, and
The Gypsy Laddie, 200 I. This leaves twelve
ballads to be considered; many are fragments of
only a few lines, others tell quite a full story.

Miss Reburn's variant of *The Bailiff's Daughter of Islington* (105) is mentioned by Child. He notes that Percy's copy contains

a few casual verbal variations, attributable to imperfect recollection of a broadside. There are much better in a copy which I have received from an Irish lady, partly made over by secondary tradition. (II, 426)

Child knew that this ballad was 'still very much sung' (II, 426), yet he printed a broadside copy. The seven stanzas from Miss Reburn may be compared with stanzas 3, 5 and 9-13 of the text printed by Child. The two opening lines of Miss Reburn's second stanza, however, have no parallel there.

1 They sent him away to a far countery
    And a 'prentice they got him bound bound
    And a 'prentice they got him bound
  Looking over the books and studying the law
    Was all that he had for to mind mind
  But the bailie's daughter of Islington
    She still ran in his mind mind
    She still ran in his mind

2 It was on a day, and a high holliday;
    Just about Lammas time time
  When all the young girls of Islington
    Got ready for to sport, and play play
  All but the bailie's fair daughter
    And she privately stole away way
    And she privately stole away

3 How far did you travel my pretty little page?
    And where were you bred and born
  In Islington kind sir he [sic] said
    Where I bore many a scorn,
    Where I bore many a [scorn]

4 Did you ever see or know
    The bailie's daughter of Islington?

She is dead sir long ago go
She is dead sir long ago

5 If she be dead and not alive
But laid in her grave so low low
Here I deliver you my milk white steed
My arrow and my bow bow
My arrow and my bow
And I will away to some strange countery
Where no man will me know know
Where no man will me know

6 She's not dead but she's alive
And standing by your side side
She's not dead but she's alive
And ready for to be your bride bride
And ready for to be your bride

7 Farewel grief and welcome joy
Ten thousand times and more more
And since we met no more we'ill part
Till time shall be no more more
Till time shall be no more

Later collectors have found examples which resemble this. It is a great pity that Miss Reburn
was not asked for the tune, for several of the
variants with tunes printed by Professor Bronson[20]
have this kind of stanza form. In Britain it
occurs in Orkney, County Galway and Aberdeenshire
(Bronson, 105 numbers 7, 8 and 13), in America in
Kentucky and Missouri (Bronson, 105 numbers 3, 5
and 4). The words of these traditional variants
repay study. Bronson's numbers 3, 4, 5 and 7
mention that this episode happened in summer,
while 8 says that it happened 'When three long
months were past and gone' and school maids had
'got leave to play' (stanza 4). In other variants
in Bronson, not ones with this stanza form, the
heat and dryness of the weather is mentioned (as
it is in Child's text) but the season is not named
as summer except in numbers 18, 19 and 20, all of

which are from Nova Scotia and all of which have
Irish place-names in the text. It is interesting
to look at Greig's variant[21] at this point, for
his examples have a stanza formation similar to
Miss Reburn's variant yet have the same words as
the English broadside printed by Child.

> And as she went along the road,
>   The weather being hot and dry.
>
> (Child 105, stanza 7)

The stanza form of Miss Reburn's variant, suggesting as it does a strong link with a melody, is
known in Ireland, Scotland and North America,
while a four-line form was also current.

Many of Miss Reburn's ballads show Scottish
connections; even when all she knew was a single
stanza it may be recognisable as part of a ballad
widely known in Scotland. This can be seen in this
fragment, which was identified by Child on Miss
Reburn's letter as *Lady Maisry* (65).

> For your sake Lady Margery
>   I'll burn kith and kin
> And for your sake Lady Margery
>   I'll burn the town you're in

This is most like 65 D, E and F; it reads like a
memory of the last two or three stanzas of these
variants run together into a single stanza. Miss
Reburn noted in her first letter that this might
be like 'Sir Walter's "When he cam to broken
brigs".' One wonders if she could be thinking of
the heading to Chapter XXXIII of *Rob Roy* for although this phrase occurs in several versions of
Lady Maisry (A, E, F and less exactly B, C and G)
these were not printed by Scott. This phrase
occurs also in other ballads, for example *Johnie
Scot* (99) and *Little Musgrave* (81), and was a
common phrase in oral tradition in lowland Scotland.

Miss Reburn's *Tam Lin* (39) is of great interest,

especially for the folklore revealed in the transformation. This is one of the ballads where she
sent a single stanza first and the rest later. It
will be seen that the changes are not significant.

> The first thing that they turned him to
>   Was to a fiery snake
> She hel[d] him fast she feared him not
>   He was one of God's own make

This is from item 8 and the longer fragment comes
from item 11.

1 To night it is a Friday night
    And tomorrow is Hallow'een
  And the Elfin train will ride along
    To mortal ken unseen

2 So hold me fast whate'er betide
    At tomorrow's set of Sun
  Nor fear the Fairy queen her wrath
    Your darling will be won

3 May she came and May she went
    And watched that Hollantide
  And held her lover fast and true
    Whatever might betide

4 The first thing that they turned him to
    Was to a bush so green
  She held him fast she feared him not
    She had her darling seen

5 The next thing that they turned him to
    Was to a fierie snake
  She held him fast she feared him not
    He was one of God's own make

6 The last thing that they turned him to
    Was to a naked man
  She held him fast she feared him not
    She had her darling won

7 Out bespoke the queen of the fairies
    Oh but she spoke angery

Had I known that late last night
Or two hours before day
I would take out his bonny bonny heart
And put in a heart of clay

In spite of occasional phrases that do not ring
true, such as 'your darling will be won', this
gives a good idea of the transformation theme of
Tam Lin. The 'fiery snake' is reminiscent of both
the 'snake' and the 'fiery brand' of other variants. 'He was one of God's own make' could have
arisen from a misunderstanding of the Scottish
'make' meaning 'mate' (see 39 E 17, G 40, H 12,
I 40). It is unusual for Tam Lin to be transformed
into a 'green bush', yet a green tree is common in
folksong to symbolise a young man,[22] occurring,
for example, in *O Waly Waly* where the girl laments,
'I leant my back against an oak, I thought it was
a trusty tree.'
  Tam Lin is a Scottish ballad, and so is *Young
Hunting* (68) of which Miss Reburn knew a dozen
lines.

She booted him, she spurred him
As if he were going to ride
With a bugle horn about his middle
And a small sword by his left side

Will your son be home today
Or will he be home tomorrow
If he does not be home in a very few days
My heart will break with sorrow

If Adam's well it was well searched
From bottom unto brim
Its there the goodly Lord would be found
Where sorely she wounded him

Professor Bronson comments on this ballad:

This Scottish ballad, if it ever had any currency
in England, seems to have left no trace there,
but to have passed directly to this country

[that is, the United States], where it has enjoyed a great vogue in our own century — at least
in the Appalachians.[23]

The first four lines may be compared with Scottish
forms of the ballad (A 12, B 11, D 9, G 2, H 4,
K 15 and Bronson's variant 34). The 'well' motif
may be found in Motherwell's variant (F 8) and in
some trans-Atlantic variants (Bronson numbers 5
stanza 9; 8.12; 9.10; 17.4 and 36.6). It is noteworthy that Bronson's number 36 could be traced to
a woman born in Ireland. Here we have among Miss
Reburn's ballads lines from one that was current
in oral tradition in early nineteenth-century
Scotland and that was also known in American tradition.

Young Beichan (53)

What would you give to a Turkish lady
    Who would set you at sweet liberty

Oh London lady is all my own
    Besides other cities two or three
But my brother William enjoys my land
    And I fear his face I shall never see

Lamkin (93)

...Was as good a mason
    As e'er laid a stone
He built a lord's castle
    But payme[nt] got none

Where is my lord
    Or is he within
He is gone o'er to England
    To wait on the King

Both of these fragments are too brief to furnish
much evidence. It is noteworthy that Lamkin's
trade is made clear although his name has disappeared; this suggests that the *Lamkin* fragment

should be placed with the Scottish — Appalachian group of versions.[24]

The Death of Queen Jane (170)

Queen Jane was in labor for six weeks & more
Till the doctors and midwives they all gave her
   o'er
There went three and three maidens there went
   three & three more
All seeking King Henry, his loss to deplore

King Henry he came and he knelt by her bed
What ails my sweet princess her eyes look so red
Nor Leeches nor midwives grim death cannot stay
And sweet Jane the Princess to the tomb is borne
   away

This is related to the versions published by Child,[25] many of which are Scottish, although it must be remembered that this ballad was often printed in the eighteenth century in England. It is clear that some of Child's variants, D, E and F, came from oral tradition and that therefore the ballad had shaken off the shackles of the eighteenth-century printed texts.

The Twa Sisters (10)

Yonder sits my father the king
   Heigho my Nannie O
And next to him my mother the queen
   And the swans swim so bonny O

This clearly belongs to the group of variants of Child 10 represented by G (Motherwell), J ('from the north of Ireland'), P (Motherwell) and Child's notes on C where he gives a single stanza of a variant with this refrain. Scott knew of this refrain, but published the *Binnorie* refrain in his *Minstrelsy*. It seems that this group of variants was drawn from oral tradition in Scotland in the early nineteenth century and that it was also part

of Irish tradition. Bronson comments on this in
his introduction to *The Two Sisters* and some of
his examples with this refrain are of Irish
descent.[26] It seems particularly sad that we do
not have Miss Reburn's tune for this for it might
have been invaluable in sorting out the different
variants of this ballad.

Fair Janet (64) ?

Fly oh fly then my sweet Willie
  Fly oh fly love and come with me
Through France and Spain and England too
  And the broad earth I would range with you

They scarcely were a league from home
  A league from home aye only three
When he heard his young son cry
  And moaning hard for his fair Ladie

. . . .
They both fell down in a deadly swoon
  And never came to life again

This contains one motif, the birth while on a
journey, which is found in several Scottish
ballads. The evidence provided by this fragment is
not specific, so only a tentative identification
may be suggested, on the grounds of stanza form,
the fatal ending and the name 'Willie'.

Lord Thomas and Lady Margaret (260)

Lord Thomas he was a gay good Lord
  Lady Margaret she loved him right well
And all for the sake of the good Lord Thom[as]
  Through the woods Lady Margaret ran wild

Here again there is very little material on which
to base any conclusions, but this stanza is so
strikingly like the first stanza of *Lord Thomas
and Lady Margaret* in the Crawfurd collection from
the south-west of Scotland as to make identification very probable.

108

Lord Thomas he was a guid Lord's son
  Lady Margeret she lo'ed him weel
An' for the sake o' guid Lord Thomas
  Lady Margeret she's gane wild[27]

The next fragment resembles Child 145 (B 4, 6),
Robin Hood and Queen Katharine, which is one of
the Robin Hood ballads so common on broadsides.

The page he chose the swiftest horse
  That ran on Dallon Lea
And he set off for Nottingham
  As fast as he could flee

The last ballad is a most strange and interesting variant of *Sir Hugh, or, The Jew's Daughter*
(155). This was a ballad of which Miss Reburn was
proud and which she remembered a great deal about.

And with regard to Hugh of Lincoln I dis-
tinctly remember the impression it made on my
mind as the ballad represented the jew's daughter as killing him for the purpose of getting
his heart's blood to concoct charms and so in
unison with the prejudice against them in those
days
    He was going to school and the morning was
wet and the jew's daughter called him in out of
the rain
    Fancy stamped the scene indelibly on my mind
so that I knew what side of the street the jew
lived on and could see the girl come outside of
the gate and call after him though the ballad
did not go into particulars   (Letter 3)

1 Child Sir Hugh was an ae ane son
    His mother she nought but he
  And he maun hie to merrie Lincoln
    To study the grammarie

2 The rain it rained owre a Lincoln town
    As the barnies they hied them on

And sweet Sir Hugh the fairest of them all
   Why lags he behind them this morn

3 The owd jew's daughter from her turret so high
   She has sweet Sir Hugh espied
And out she cam at her father's gate
   And him she desired to bide

4 Come hither come hither thou pretty little Bairn
   Cried the jew's daughter so fause & fair
Come hither come hither thou pretty little barn
   With the gowden gowden hair

5 Sweet Sir Hugh him she wyled in
   For a christened bairn is he
And the warlock airts o her owd jew father
   Writ in christened bluid maun be

6 Sweet Sir Hugh he ne'er gat hame
   To the mother who luved him sa dear
And she has wandered ower a the land
   Tidings of sweet Sir Hugh to speer

7 She wandered East and she wandered West
   And she prayed at our Ladie's shrine
Oh Mother dear of the fair child Christ
   Restore to my arms mine

8 Sweet ladie Maisrie, & fair ladie Maisrie
   Thy Sir Hugh he will yet be found
But only to have his faire bodie
   Placed in holy ground

9 The ladie Maisrie as she neared her castell door
   And before the cocks they did crow
She was aware of a shining light
   And her sweet Sir Hugh she did know

10 Oh sweet mother dear and sweet mother mine
   And mother mine for ever mair
Get ready get ready a winding sheet
   To wrap my bodie fair

11 For my bodie it lies in our Ladie's drawwell
   By the jew's daughter it was thrown

> And she lapped my heart's bluid drop by drop
> And she heard my heart's last moan

12 The ladie Maisrie has made the winding sheet
 And her tears they did fall like rain
 And in the churchyard of merrie Lincoln town
 They have his fair bodie lain

13 Now the Mass is sung and the bells are rung
 And the Acolytes are all gone away
 And sweet Sir Hugh he lies in holy ground
 Until the judgement day

Miss Reburn knew that there was something unusual about the language of this ballad, for she commented:

> It is only through Scotland that we know what we do of the old English ballads you may see by the orthography of the words such English as Sir Hugh was never spoken in my country but it is so in many districts of England yet therefore we lack the very old form   (Letter 6)

One must reserve judgement about this ballad; in particular one notes that the Scottish spellings could have come from a written source; they are different in quality from the misunderstanding of 'make' in *Tam Lin* which clearly suggests oral transmission.

These then are Miss Reburn's ballads. They vary in quality and many pieces are but fragments yet they represent the kind of repertoire that might have been found in Meath in the 1860s. A consideration of the value of this material must take into account what Miss Reburn herself felt about her ballads. As we have seen she thought they were from oral tradition, yet many of them are derived from printed texts of the first twenty years of the nineteenth century. Miss Reburn knew of some of the printed collections, for she commented,

> I often heard of Percy's but never had the

111

pleasure of seeing his Relics nor all of Sir
Walter's   (Letter 4)

She was convinced that her ballads did not come
out of such collections:

> ...I think I may venture to assert that the
> *words* I send belong to a version of these sub-
> jects that have never been in print As we had
> in our home in Ireland a large well bound volume
> of old ballads published in 1775 but in a dif-
> ferent version   (Letter 1)

Collections such as these do not seem to have been
a source for her material, for *Charms of Melody* is
in a rather different category. Indeed it is difficult to classify this series; it drew on chapbook
material yet could not in fairness be called a
series of chapbooks nor yet is it a volume of
collected ballads comparable with Scott's *Minstrelsy*.

What kind of people would have sung songs such
as these? It has long been felt, and has most
authoritatively been shown by Professor Bronson[28]
that people of all classes, not only the poorer
farmers, enjoyed ballads in the eighteenth and
nineteenth centuries. It is therefore interesting
to find a voice from the nineteenth century main-
taining the same view.

> But Professor there is one item I wish to advert
> to and please do not think me rather sensitive
> on that point — your circular says that it may
> be that people of some education may know some
> old ballads — I am from there, and to the manner
> born, and know of what I speak, Now, if you
> Professor, will please to notice, the higher
> classes, as well as the simple lower classes,
> retain a fund of past time ideas, and phrase-
> ology, and that it is only those *Noveau Riches*
> people, who discard it, I know for one that Miss
> Edgeworth and Mrs S.C.Hall were particulary

112

attached to these selfsame old ballads

(Letter 2)

The difficulty arises when we come to ask what
Miss Reburn would have called a ballad — her
definition, we assume, would include all that she
sent to Child as 'traditionary Ballads' while ex-
cluding 'all the modern Scotch songs' and 'Moore's
Melodies'.[29] It is clear that Miss Reburn thought
of her ballads as being sung, 'Everyone sung them
everyone knew fragments of them',[29] and in this
she approached modern definitions of the ballad.
Some of her ballads, for example *The Bailiff's
Daughter of Islington* (155), show by internal
evidence that they must have been associated with
a melody. Some of her ballads are clearly from
oral tradition and many of these, as we have seen,
are related to Scottish ballads or to Scottish
forms of ballads known both north and south of the
Border. Again, Miss Reburn's own comments are
pertinent:

> It is only through Scotland that we know what we
> do of the old English ballads   (Letter 6)

> We knew nothing of England of her songs feelings
> & domestic life only the Irish Sea separated us
> but the wall of China could not keep us asunder
> more effectually   (Letter 3)

In view of the possibility that the Scotch-Irish
who emigrated from Ulster to the Southern Appalachians may have brought many Scottish ballads
with them,[30] it is interesting to see that Miss
Reburn thought that 'the descendants of Protest-
ants from the North of Ireland' might 'take an
interest' (Letter 7), although in fact she did not
manage to obtain any contributions from her Northern Irish friends.

This then is what Miss Reburn thought about her
material. She knew fragments of a body of song
that everyone, of higher as well as lower class,

113

sang in her childhood in Ireland, as far as she
was aware her ballads did not come from printed
books, and their connections were with Scotland
rather than with England. Those of her ballads
that can reasonably be said to be from oral tradition show a marked resemblance to variants from
Scotland. Up to this point we may agree with Miss
Reburn's views, but she also sent Child several
ballads that are close to print and some completely
non-traditional pieces that she thought were old
ballads. However, we must not be too hard on her;
she made no pretentions to being a scholar, and
where her texts seem like chapbook examples we
must remember that many ballads were transmitted
by chapmen.[31] The mixture of traditional and non-
traditional in her repertoire is not surprising;
these were the ballads that people enjoyed, without stopping to enquire where the songs came from.
The value of Miss Reburn's ballads for us today is
twofold: those of her ballads which seem to be
traditional enlarge our knowledge, especially as
they suggest that some Scottish ballads were known
in the English-speaking part of Ireland in the
nineteenth century, and her repertoire as a whole
is representative of the songs that were enjoyed
by all classes in County Meath when Miss Reburn
was a girl.

Acknowledgements:

   *Material from Volume XVIII of the Child MSS
(25241.47F*) is published by permission of the
Harvard College Library. I would like to thank the
Executive Committee of the Radcliffe Institute,
Harvard University, for their generosity in giving
me a Fellowship that enabled me to undertake this
study.*

APPENDIX

G.L.KITTREDGE ARRANGED AND numbered the items sent
to Child by Miss Reburn, items 1-7 being her
letters and 8-11 consisting of song texts. Item 8
contains eighteen fragments, some of them later
enlarged, and seems to have been sent with the
first letter. The fragments on this sheet which
appear also as parts of longer texts are not
listed separately, but are shown after the main
texts following the letters 'frag.'. The addition
of a letter to the Child number indicates that
Child printed Miss Reburn's text.

Item 8   CHILD NUMBER

 3 Lady Maisry (1 stanza)   65
 5 Young Johnstone (1 stanza)   88
 9 Betsy Is a Beauty Fair (2 lines)
11 Siúil a Rúin (1 stanza)
15 Robin Hood and Queen Katherine (1 stanza) 145
16 The Cruel Mother (1 stanza)   20 M
17 'Straight to Paris...' (1 stanza)
18 Lord Thomas and Lady Margaret (1 stanza) 260

Item 9

 1 Edom o' Gordon (26 stanzas); frag.no 7   178
 2 Sir James the Rose (12 stanzas);
    frag.no 14   213
 3 Earl Walter (10 stanzas)   cf. 63
 4 The Vanquished King (14 stanzas)
 5 The Water King (10 lines)
 6 Young Beichan (6 lines)   53
 7 Lamkin (2 stanzas)   93

Item 10

 1 Fair Annie (5 stanzas)   62 G
 2 The Bailiff's Daughter of Islington
    (6 or 7 stanzas); frag.no 2   105

3 Young Hunting (3 stanzas); frag.no 10   68
4 Queen Eleanor's Confession (4 stanzas);
     frag.no 13   156
5 The Cruel Brother (14 stanzas);
     frag.no 6   11 J
6 The Gay Goshawk (4 stanzas); frag.no 1   96 F
7 The Death of Queen Jane (2 stanzas)   170
8 Fair Janet (10 lines)   64 ?

Item 11

1 Sir Hugh, or, The Jew's Daughter
    (13 stanzas)   155
2 The Gypsy Laddie (8 stanzas); frag.no 8   200 I
3 Fair Rosamund betrayed to the Queen
    (14 stanzas)
4 Little Musgrave and Lady Barnard
    (2 stanzas)   81 N
5 Tam Lin (7 stanzas); frag.no 4   39

Fair Rosamund foretells her fate (6 stanzas), frag.
no 12, and *The Twa Sisters* (1 stanza), Child 10,
occur in letter 2, which also includes a fragment
of *Sir Hugh, or, The Jew's Daughter* of which a
longer text is found in item 11. *The Cruel Stepmother* (about 8 double stanzas) occurs in letter 7.

7. THE SCOTTISH ELEMENT IN TRADITIONAL BALLADS COLLECTED IN AMERICA

Herschel Gower

NUMEROUS ESSAYS BY many hands have attempted to evaluate the Scottish contributions to early American tradition. A number of historians have dealt with the political and ethnological patterns which the Scots and Ulster Scots established in the Old Southwest during the eighteenth and early nineteenth centuries, particularly in the vast Appalachian area extending from the western borders of Pennsylvania in the north to the Alabama highlands in the south. The proverbially shrewd and frugal Scotsman has sometimes been typified as the pioneer American and called the 'cutting edge' of the frontier during the early development of the nation. To him have been attributed dramatic concepts of political freedom; he has been charged with carrying on the tradition of blood feuds and clan warfare that had engaged his forebears for generations in Scotland; and he has been praised for promulgating the Calvinist gospel, saving souls in the dark backwoods, and setting up log cabin 'colleges' in the forest clearings.

His descendants have often pointed proudly to their Scottish ancestry — whether Highland, Lowland, or Ulster in origin — and have flattered him, tended to romanticise his memory, and occasionally have made claims for him that were clearly extravagant. But objective and impartial investigations of more recent date have not refuted the major claims. In 1954, for example, the several studies published in the *William and Mary Quarterly* again underscored the fact that Scottish contributions to early America were both actual and concrete, that Scotland and the Scots were notable forces in the political, commercial, and religious life of the young nation, and that America, for any number of reasons, has benefited by the presence of Scottish blood. Another work of importance was published in 1956 by the American Historical Association, a study by Ian Charles Cargill Graham entitled *Colonists from Scotland: Emigration to North America, 1707-1783*, which is by far the most reliable survey of Scottish economic and social contributions to America during the eighteenth century.[1]

One contribution, however, has somehow been neglected. Perhaps the difficulty of the task and the scarcity of concrete evidence are sufficiently valid reasons for the delay. Whatever the causes, it is the purpose of this study to define and discuss some of the contributions made by Scotland and the Scots to the oral literature of the United States; to show, specifically, the extension of Scottish minstrelsy to those areas of America which received, nourished, and adopted the songs and ballads as part of the popular traditional literature of succeeding generations.

Many early writers in America lumped all the Scots together without discrimination — Highlanders, Lowlanders, and Scotch-Irish — and spoke of them collectively. On the other hand, colonial records sometimes referred to the Scots from Ulster as 'Irish', a name which they resented and which caused them to affirm that they were not Irish but people who 'frequently ventured our all for the British Crown and Liberties against the Irish Papists'. When writing about the Scottish contributions to America, other writers have found it more convenient to focus their studies entirely on these Ulster Scots or Scotch-Irish, with secondary consideration for the Lowland and Highland stock.[2] Yet it has been reckoned that by actual numbers the Scots proper were in stronger force than those from Ulster, the native Scots having been about one-third greater in the

118

colonial population than the Scotch-Irish.[3]

To understand fully the influences loosely
classified as 'Scotch' by the early writers, one
must glance at the Scottish scene at the time of
the main stream of emigration from 1707 to 1783.
There we can see the presence of two distinct
cultures: that of the Celtic tradition from the
Highlands and Western Isles, expressed in Gaelic
speech, and that designated as the Lowland Scots
culture, expressed in the language of Lowland
Scotland. In the course of the seventeenth century,
because of the extensive grants of Irish lands to
Scotsmen (the Plantation of Ulster), a large in-
flux of Scottish settlers into Ulster took place.
This colonisation continued into the eighteenth
century, particularly after the Jacobite rebellions of 1715 and 1745. Eventually a very large
number of these same Ulster Scots emigrated to
America, bringing with them their distinctive
Scotch-Irish culture and making it impossible for
historians to differentiate between the influence
of this group and that of settlers who emigrated
directly from Scotland. Therefore, for the purpose
of this study, 'Scots' refers to the language of
Lowland Scotland and that of the Ulster Scots.
'Gaelic', on the other hand, is used for the
language of the Celtic areas of the Highlands and
the Western Islands.

When the American Historical Association published its report in 1931 on the Scottish population in America at the time of the first national census in 1790, it used a slightly different nomenclature for the three main groups. For
example, both Highland and Lowland names were
taken into account in the study, but the percent-
ages for the two groups were ultimately totalled
under 'Scotch'. Those from Ulster were included
under the broader term 'Ulster Irish', which
allowed for the 'Scotch-Irish' but separated them
at the same time from the South (Celtic) Irish.[4]

This method of determining the number of Scots and their kin by an analysis of distinctive surnames cannot be accepted as infallible. On the other hand, it seems the most ingenious approach so far devised to supply, at least in theory, the information about national backgrounds of the population in 1790 that was not supplied in fact. The subtotals in the report, though at best only estimates, are valuable indicators of population, and they invariably point to large numbers of Scots in Virginia, North Carolina, and Pennsylvania — all three of which are key states in folksong contributions.

What then were the summary findings in the report? Out of a total white population of 3,172,444 in the United States in 1790, there were 263,330 inhabitants who by birth or ancestry could be called either Highland or Lowland Scots. Comparatively speaking, these Scots represented only 8.3 per cent of the total population, a figure surprisingly low for all the states and far below the 60.9 per cent represented by the English.[5] But the Scottish ratio increases rapidly if mainland Scots are combined with those from Ulster. That is, 8.3 added to 6.0 (Ulster Scots)[6] amounts to 14.3, the possible percentage of all Scottish stock in the United States. With that figure, the national ratio of all Scots to all English would be about one to four.

There is another (perhaps even more important) consideration, for regionalism has been a major factor in the cultural composition of America. What then of geographic distribution? How was the Scottish population distributed among the several states? Of the 263,330 estimated Highland and Lowland Scots, only one sixth of them had gone to New England, while 83.8 per cent had settled in the states south of New England. Almost two thirds had settled

in the five states of Virginia, North Carolina,

Pennsylvania, New York, and South Carolina, named in the order of their importance. Particularly large numbers...were in Virginia (17 per cent), North Carolina (16 per cent), and Pennsylvania (14 per cent).[7]

That is to say that 47 per cent of the total Scottish population of America was concentrated in these last three states alone. Furthermore, it is reckoned that 10 per cent of the total white population of Tennessee and Kentucky in 1790 was of Scottish ancestry and that Georgia was even higher with its 15.5 per cent.[8]

These last figures deal only with the Scots from Scotland — those with distinctively Highland and Lowland names. Those from Ulster were reckoned under a separate grouping; and yet it is convenient to say here that Ulster Scots were also high in Pennsylvania, Georgia, South Carolina, Kentucky, and Tennessee. Usually there was a

fair similarity between the Ulster Irish and the Scotch measures, though the latter is in general about a third higher.[9]

In other words, the Scots and Ulster Scots seem to have settled usually in the same geographical areas. Being of the same blood and ultimate origin, they would be expected to combine forces, so to speak, in establishing pronounced cultural patterns if they found homes in outlying, thinly populated sections where other patterns were not already established; and if they remained sufficiently isolated in the new country.

If more complete records were available for the hundreds of early Presbyterian congregations — especially those beginning in New Jersey and spreading southwestwards in a fairly well-defined arc through the mountains and valleys of western Pennsylvania, Virginia, and North Carolina[10] — then 'Scottishness' might be better evaluated. The

Presbyterian Church would certainly have been a cultural, as well as religious bastion, unconsciously preserving to some extent a number of folkways by virtue of its holding together in its congregations a body of people with the same background.

To what extent Lowland and Ulster Scots maintained their distinctive speech has seldom been intimated by contemporary records, though the Highlander is known to have kept Scottish Gaelic alive in North Carolina for several generations and to have listened to sermons preached in Gaelic from as early as 1736 through the Revolution, and as late as the middle of the nineteenth century.[11] But most of the cultural details are lacking for the Scots as a whole; the dominant English, who were the record-keepers and statisticians in Britain, assumed the same role in America. They either neglected cultural factors that were not English or blithely underestimated them as they had been wont to do at home.

Politically, the rough-and-ready Scots were resented by the policy-making tidewater Englishmen; in fact the Virginia gentry looked upon these men in the hilly and mountainous sections as 'banditti' who drank too much liquor, held scant respect for English law and order, and established in the hills a 'Mac-ocracy' of their own.[12] Their increasing numbers in the uplands of North Carolina from 1731 to 1775 made the Piedmont populous, the collection of taxes a hazardous task for the agents of royal governors, and the balance of power difficult to maintain.[13]

By 1776 it is estimated that there were at least five hundred 'Scotch-Irish' communities throughout colonial America, a number that may or may not include the two other divisions of Scots. Of these communities, only seventy were in New England. The rest were distributed:

...40 to 50 in New York, 50 to 60 in New Jersey, over 130 in Pennsylvania and Delaware, over 100 in Virginia, Maryland and Tennessee, 50 in North Carolina, and about 70 in South Carolina and Georgia.[14]

Although this informal estimate makes no attempt to count heads or to give geographical distribution within the individual colony, it would certainly agree in general with the conclusions independently reached by the American Historical Association in its analysis of surnames. Quite possibly these Scottish and Scotch-Irish communities in the 1790 population were more poorly served by the first census — because of the geographical remoteness of their habitations and the unsettled character of the frontier — than the English settlements nearer the capital and counting house. It is far more difficult to count sheep in the hills than in the fank, and there were innumerable Scots settled in the hills by 1790.

Whatever their reasons for leaving Scotland — whether the Covenanter troubles, the rebellions of 1715 and 1745, the highland clearances and the breaking up of the clan system, resentment by the Irish in Ulster, or the changing economy in the eighteenth century — the Scots who came to America came in numbers second only to the English. By nature and constitution they were equipped for the demands of the New World; physically, they were the tallest race in Europe. Of these backwoodsmen — speakers of Scots or Scottish Gaelic — Constance Rourke has said:

With an untouched wilderness on the horizon, they moved onward and became the first explorers of the dark and bloody ground.[15]

About them and their traditional literature Sir Walter Scott made a knowledgeable prediction when he imagined the song of an uprooted Scotsman in the New World:

A mellow voice Fitz-Eustace had,
The air he chose was wild and sad;
Such have I heard, in Scottish land,
Rise from the busy harvest band,
When falls before the mountaineer,
On Lowland plains, the ripen'd ear.
Now one shrill voice the notes prolong,
Now a wild chorus swells the song:
Oft have I listen'd, and stood still,
As it came soften'd up the hill,
And deemed it the lament of men
Who languish'd for their native glen;
And thought how sad would be such sound
On Susquehana's swampy ground,
Kentucky's wood-encumber'd brake
Or wild Ontario's boundless lake,
Where heart-sick exiles, in the strain,
Recall'd fair Scotland's hills again.[16]

This is the prediction of a poet schooled in the ways of folklore, a seer whose insight was both natural and imaginative when he spoke of people and their songs. Scott's prophecy has now been proved valid, for Scottish songs and music have indeed been discovered in those places he imagined — in the backwoods and byways of the American continent where the descendants of kinsmen and clansmen have kept alive an ancient heritage.

Although Gaelic Scotland is responisble for many fine tunes in North America, the texts of Gaelic songs can still be heard only in Canada, particularly Cape Breton Island, Nova Scotia, where the literature of the Scottish Gael is a living tradition in the country districts. Gaelic has not survived in North Carolina, and the culture of the Highlands, except for the tunes, seems

124

generally to have been dissipated in the United
States, where anglicisation of the Gael moved at a
remarkable pace.

On the other hand, survivals of Lowland Scots
language and culture have been more numerous and
often clearly distinguishable. On the Pennsylvania
frontier at the occurrence of the Whiskey Rebellion in 1793-1794, David Bruce was writing what
was certainly authentic Scottish verse. He found
that people distinguished by the name of *Scots-
Irish* were the most numerous audience he had in
western Pennsylvania. About whiskey, a popular
Scottish product, he wrote for a corps of readers
who thirstily admired the commodity:

> Great Pow'r, that warms the heart and liver,
> And puts the bluid a' in a fever,
> If dull and heartless I am ever
>   A blast o' thee
> Maks me as blyth, and brisk, and clever
>   As ony bee.[17]

During that same period, Hugh Henry Brackenridge
of Pittsburgh wrote verses in Scots and made his
famous character, Duncan, in *Modern Chivalry*,
speak the language common to Ulster and Lowland
Scotland:

> The dialect of Duncan, which is called braid
> Scots, or what is the same thing, the Scots-
> Irish, was my native dialect.[18]

His son, H.M.Brackenridge, recalled his grand-
mother's Scottish speech and her stories about
Scotland in the early eighteenth century — 'about
the Duke of Argyle's castle and its scenery'.[19]
All the family had a taste for the Scottish poets
from Gavin Douglas to Robert Burns, and there were
plenty of neighbours to share their enthusiasm.

Aside from these literary productions, there
existed other survivals on a folk level in the
Southern Highlands, where generally the oldest

speech forms, both English and Scottish, have been retained. Among the American collectors of mountain dialect was Josiah H.Combs, who contributed the following notes:

> In West Virginia and in the Shenandoah Valley of Virginia numerous Scottish survivals are found..
> ..A few words of more or less Scottish tincture follow: *bonnie; cadgy* (pro. *caigy*), wanton, lustful; *ferment* (*ferminst*), near, or just beyond; *gin,* if; *nee*(*d*)*cessity; sich* (*sech*) *an' sich* (also Elizabethan); *trollop.*[20]

Although the yield is sometimes plainly Scottish, it is very often faintly Scottish in word lists from the Appalachian area. Both types should be considered, however, for the Scots can very probably be given part of the credit for the importation of 'Elizabethan' English to the Southern Highlands. Ironically, it was Scotland which retained in common currency many of the older words and expressions that had been dropped in England by the eighteenth century. In fact, it can be argued that from the time of James I the literature of England had devastating effects in Scotland. The best example of this, and the one often cited, is the King James Bible. Lacking their own translation, the Scots embraced the Scriptures in English and became bilingual in a very real sense. They retained their native tongue for everyday use — in the field or by the fireside. But they resorted to English on Sunday, or when the occasion demanded high and righteous diction. Robert Burns's shift from Scots to English in the latter part of 'The Cotter's Saturday Night' is a case in point.

Particularly in the cities was the metamorphosis apparent. As late as 1822, Sir Walter Scott recalled the changes:

> Scotch was a language which we have heard spoken

by the learned and the wise and witty and the
accomplished...You remember how well Mrs Murray
Keith, the late Lady Dumfries, my poor Mother
and other ladies of that day spoke their native
language — it was different from English as the
Venetian is from the Tuscan dialect of Italy
but it never occured [sic] to any one that the
Scotish any more than the Venetian was more
vulgar than those who spoke the purer and more
classical. But that is all gone and the remem-
brance will be drowned with us the elders of
this existing generation...So glides this world
away...21

Here Sir Walter is lamenting the passing of Scots
in *educated* circles. In those societies to which
the ballads retreated and in which they were continued, the diction remained far richer than the
language of Scott's intimates in Edinburgh. Every
generation announces that Scots is dying, but
Johnny Gibb of Gushetneuk was written fifty years
after Sir Walter's lamentation, and *Eppie Elrick*
was produced in 1956; both of these are just as
rich as the Scots spoken by the older generation
mentioned by Sir Walter. The ballads, on the other
hand, being 'national' and generally serious in
tone, came under the influences of anglicisation;
their texts revealed a 'standard' Scots diction
which was undoubtedly affected by many of the
collectors. Then by transplantation to America
they changed more rapidly, for the Scots in the
New World were surrounded by English as the dominant language culture. It would be practically
impossible to maintian the Scottish tongue and the
distinctive vocabulary of Scottish speech for many
generations in a cultural climate that was pre-
dominately English. Whereas in Scotland there was
a national pride and a more immediate cultural
context that retarded dissolution, in America the
popular literature came under the influences of

English speech. To survive, the songs were forced to alter under the demands of a new, formative society.

If Francis J.Child had been allowed more time for the completion of his labours, we would almost certainly be better informed about the Scottish ballads in his collection. He might have been persuaded to make generalisations about the Scottish texts, as a result of his long study, that no ballad editor has since been willing to hazard — if any has indeed been qualified.[22] Gavin Greig was the best of the later collectors in Scotland, but Greig himself died in the very midst of his studies, leaving only brief notes and three or four essays limited in scope. These dealt mainly with balladry in Aberdeenshire, not in Scotland as a whole. So the comprehensive work dealing with Scottish balladry as a separate study has yet to be written. It is significant, however, that Child called his collection *English and Scottish Popular Ballads*, nor merely *English Popular Ballads*. Yet when Cecil Sharp came to America and recorded folksongs in the South, he published the traditional ballads of England *and* Scotland as *English Folk Songs from the Southern Appalachians*. By so doing, Sharp perpetrated a certain amount of confusion — however much we respect his significant contributions to folksong — and the Scottish content in both tunes and texts has usually been minimised because of Sharp's neglect. Ballad scholars simply have not designated clearly the Scottish corpus in America. Therefore, because American versions of the Scottish ballads will be discussed later in this study, it is necessary now to attempt a definition of the native Scottish ballad as it is found in Professor Child's collection, and to supply suf- ficient reasons for regarding it as distinctively

Scottish rather than English. Those examples in
the Child canon which particularly concern us here
— those for which there is convincing Scottish
evidence — may be determined by the following
criteria:

I. Ballads which have been collected only in
Scotland; which were never recorded in the oral
tradition of England; which Professor Child and
his successors have not traced to English sources.

II. Ballads which have a basis in Scottish
history; which relate historical incidents from
Scotland in their stories; and which also qualify
for I, above.

III. Ballads which have generally had wide currency in Scottish tradition, including language
and idiom, with only limited currency in other
parts of Britain.

IV. Ballads believed to be of English origin, but
so long in currency in Scotland that they were
obviously 'naturalised' there before being carried
to America.

This classification is based on geographical
considerations — on the fact that certain ballads
were commonplace within the geographical bound-
aries of Scotland *over a long period of time* and
for that reason can logically be called Scottish.

Additional criteria may also be established,
particularly in regard to ballad texts:

A. Ballads which the early collectors, scholars,
and commentators point to and discuss as Scottish.

B. Ballads which reveal Scottish place names,
personal names, or other Scottish associations in
the earliest recorded texts.

C. Ballads which were taken first from the lips
of singers native to Scotland or singers known to
be of a Scottish background.

D. Ballads which used Lowland Scots vernacular in the earliest recorded texts.

These two sets of criteria do not pretend to set up an infallible method for determining national ballad origins. Nor are they definitive in all cases. They are offered merely as indicators, as points of definition when the Scottish ballad is discussed.[23] Thus the following titles, with the numbers assigned by Child, may be considered a *primary group of Scottish ballads collected in America:*

- 3. The Fause Knight Upon the Road
- 7. Earl Brand; or, The Douglas Tragedy
- 13. Edward
- 17. Hind Horn
- 27. The Whummil Bore
- 36. Thomas Rymer
- 38. The Wee, Wee Man
- 40. The Queen of Elfan's Nourice
- 49. The Twa Brothers
- 51. Lizie Wan
- 58. Sir Patrick Spens
- 62. Fair Annie
- 68. Young Hunting
- 76. The Lass of Roch Royal
- 77. Sweet William's Ghost
- 87. Prince Robert
- 99. Johnie Scot
- 114. Johnie Cock
- 173. Mary Hamilton
- 181. The Bonny Earl of Murray
- 188. Archie o Cawfield
- 199. The Bonnie House o Airlie
- 200. The Gypsy Laddie
- 201. Bessy Bell and Mary Gray
- 210. Bonnie James Campbell
- 214. The Braes of Yarrow
- 218. The False Lover Won Back
- 221. Katherine Jaffray

226. Lizie Lindsay
240. The Rantin' Laddie
275. Get Up and Bar the Door
293. John of Hazelgreen
299. The Trooper and the Maid

For one reason or another, several of the best-known Scottish ballads failed by a margin to qualify for this first grouping.[24] An example is 'Tam Lin', the A version in Child being one of the finest of all recorded ballad texts. But because 'Tam Lin' cannot be said to have become a part of American tradition — the circumstances were questionable under which it was recorded — it is not considered here. Other examples, where evidence so far points to only a limited currency in American tradition, are:

183. Willie MacIntosh
213. Sir James the Rose
215. Rare Willie Drowned in Yarrow
217. The Broom of Cowdenknowes
225. Rob Roy
233. Andrew Lammie
236. The Laird of Drum

These have been collected only a few times in the United States, although it is quite possible that they were better known a century ago.

In reference to the primary list, it will be noted that thirty-three ballads meet the full canon. This is a relatively high number in view of the fact that the entire corpus of Child ballads so far collected in America numbers slightly over one hundred. By these first figures it can be estimated that approximately one third of America's traditional British balladry came here directly or indirectly from Scotland. Almost all these thirty-three ballads are found *only* in Scotland and America, with a few occurrences in Ireland.[25]

After the primary list, there is justification

for adding other titles and for formulating a
secondary group, for there are numerous instances
where American versions are closer to those found
in Scotland than those collected in England. These
nine titles are suggested:

    12. Lord Randal
    26. The Twa Corbies
    63. Child Waters
    65. Lady Maisry
    73. Lord Thomas and Fair Annet
    93. Lamkin
   110. The Knight and the Shepherd's Daughter
   243. James Harris; or, The Demon Lover
   274. Our Goodman

It is hoped that these groups will be accepted
as a firm corpus of Scottish ballads in America
and that there will be sufficient reasons for
future collectors to designate them as Scottish —
not as English or simply British.

It is also to the point to question the popular
assumption that Scotland and America received most
of their best ballads from England. True, there
was borrowing back and forth across the border.
But in the eighteenth century when the antiquar-
ians became interested in unrecorded literature,
Percy, an Englishman, ransacked Scotland for traditional materials which he failed to find in
England. For example, it was his Scottish corre-
spondents who provided him with these examples of
the 'classic' ballad:

    13. Edward
    58. Sir Patrick Spens
    73. Lord Thomas and Fair Annet
    77. Sweet William's Ghost
    83. Gil Morrice
    84. Sir John Grehme and Barbara Allan
    94. Young Waters
   155. Sir Hugh; or, The Jew's Daughter

132

Historically the Scots seem to have had good sense
about what makes a convincing ballad; they seem to
have known what elements are necessary to tell a
successful story; and they usually had at hand a
fitting combination of words and music. In fact,
most ballad scholars have continued to ask: Why
are Scots ballads usually so much better than
English? Why does Scotland preserve longer and
less corrupt texts? Why are the Northern tunes
generally better than the Southern?

Certain ballads show distinguishing marks of
the native Scots character: a sense of reticence,
a natural reluctance to speak of or display
emotion, a superb gift of understatement. For example, the verb *love* is practically never used in
ordinary Scots speech. Two lassies will discuss
whether they 'like' their sweethearts. One may
admit that she 'likes' Jock, which her friend will
understand to mean that she is passionately in
love with him and means to marry him. More often
she will say that she 'gets on fine with Jock', or
that he is 'nae bad'. Jock will describe his Jean
in similar terms to his friends. If he tells them
Jean is a 'fine lassie', they will understand that
he has completely lost his head over her. This
understatement is very obvious in Scots poetry as
a whole and of course in the ballads. It is
exactly the same quality that makes the latter
stanzas of 'Sir Patrick Spens' the moving part of
the ballad, and no Scotsman will ever miss the
implications of

Laith, laith were our guid Scots lords...
O lang, lang may their ladies sit...

or the understatement of the Border Widow lamenting

But think na ye my hairt was sair
When I laid the moul' on his yellow hair...

Add to these examples the bare dialogue of the
'Twa Corbies' and a thousand other poems and
ballads which are obviously stamped as Scots because of the terse style, the paring away of every
irrelevant detail, and the powerful understatement.
(Hear, for example, another child of the Scottish
ballad family — the anti-Polaris marching song of
the Holy Loch sitters-down — which states with
perfect brevity, 'You canny spend a dollar when
ye're deid'.)

The American ballad singer, unacquainted with
printed texts and usually unmindful of how his
predecessor came by his songs, shares with all
other traditional singers a common disregard for
folksong origins. 'It was my mother's song,' he
may tell you, 'and she got it from her mother.'
Frequently he will say he learned the song from an
uncle, or a neighbour in the next county, or a
travelling pedlar 'who had a lot of songs'. Occasionally, however, the collectors have been able
to track down and call by name the singer who
brought the ballad from Britain to America. The
editor of two Virginia collections, Arthur Kyle
Davis, Jr., furnished full documentation, whenever
possible, on how the songs came to his own region.
For example, in his headnote to 'Johnie Cock',
Davis commented:

Mrs. Dever's version of 'Lord Thomas and Fair
Eleanor' can be traced back to an old Scotchman
in Highland County years ago. Possibly 'Johnie
Cock' came from the same source.[27]

The collectors usually arrive at answers less
concrete than these, however; most of the ballads
appear to have circulated in the Appalachians too
long for the singers to remember the Old World

connections. Anyway, it is their notion that the songs are 'for singin' and no for readin',' as Mrs Hogg forcefully told Sir Walter Scott, and they have kept them alive by observing this dictum. It is someone else's notion that a song needs to be identified and annotated. The singer is not interested in the study of oral literature; he accepts or rejects a song on its basic credentials: an appealing tune and a good story. Annotation is the business of the man with books — not the minstrel or the ballad singer.

On the other hand, careful collectors are interested in the circumstances of the appearance of the ballad in America — the origin of the text and tune — and their analyses frequently make valuable contributions to the cultural history of a region. Sometimes they publish what might be called for classification purposes an 'emigrant' text, by which is meant a Child ballad which has come recently to America on the lips of an emigrant and which still retains its Scottish diction and its native idiom. On the printed page it is recognised at once for what it is — a new arrival that has not become Americanised. Davis, in *Traditional Ballads of Virginia*, printed 'Get Up and Bar the Door' as recited by Mr Robert Fleming, who learned the song in Scotland when he was a boy and remembered parts of it in dialect fifty years later in Virginia. Some of Barry's best texts in *British Ballads from Maine* were emigrant in origin, having been recorded from Mrs James McGill of Kirkcudbrightshire, who had settled some years earlier (about 1911) in New Brunswick and who still sang in Scots diction. Her brief version of 'The Rantin' Laddie' contains a refrain not attached to the ballad in other collected texts:

Aft hae I played at the cards an' dice
  For the love o' a rantin' laddie, O,
But noo I maun sit in the ingle neuk,
  An' by-lo a bastard babbie O.

REFRAIN

Sing hush-a-by, an' hush-a-by,
   An' hush-a-by-lo babbie, O,
O hush-a-by, an' hush-a-by,
   An' hush-a-by, wee babbie O.

Sing hush-a-by, an' hush-a-by,
   An' hush-a-by-lo babbie, O,
O had your tongue, ma ain wee wean,
   An A gae a sook o' the pappie, O.[28]

Mrs McGill's first stanza is also the first in
Combs's version from West Virginia, but in the
Combs stanza standard English diction has been
substituted for Scots and the 'O' endings, more
often retained in Britain than in America, have
been dropped. *Ingle neuk* becomes *fireboard* in West
Virginia; *by-lo* becomes the more usual verb *rock*;
and *rantin'* is left out of this stanza (probably
for metrical purposes) although it appears later.
Here is how Combs presented the opening stanza of
'The Rantin' Laddie' from West Virginia:

Oft have I played at cards and dice,
   For the love of my laddie;
But now I must sit at my father's fireboard,
   And rock my bastard baby.[29]

Other Combs stanzas follow the Child A in narrative construction; thus, juxtaposed, they present
a good example of the changes in diction (and
spelling) from Scotland to America:

Child A (2)

For my father he will not me own,
   And my mother she neglects me,
And a' my friends hae lightlyed me,
   And their servants they do slight me.

Combs (2)

My father he does but slight me,
   And my mother she does but scorn me,

136

And all my friends they do make light of me,
And all the servants they do sneer at me.

And the following stanzas reflect somewhat the
same transitions:

Child A (3)

But had I a servant at my command,
As aft times I've had many,
That wad rin wi a letter to bonnie Glenswood,
Wi a letter to my rantin laddie!

Combs (4)

But had I one of my father's servants,
For he has so many,
That will go to the eastern shore
With a letter to the rantin laddie.

The Combs text was sung by Mrs Nora Edman of
Big Springs, Calhoun County, West Virginia. The
collector supplied no notes about the song other
than the name of the singer and her place of
residence. It would appear that this version of
'The Rantin' Laddie' was at least second or third
generation in America; certainly it had not as
recently come from Scotland (or Scottish sources)
as Mrs McGill's or Mr Fleming's ballads. It had
already been naturalised when Mrs Edman offered it
to Professor Combs.

A particularly fine emigrant version of 'The
Bonny Earl of Murray' was recorded in Wisconsin in
1906 and later printed in the *Journal of American
Folklore*. The singer was a Scots woman visiting in
America, and the collector noted that she could
neither read nor write. She had come from Dumfries
in the Scottish Border Country, where she learned
the song in oral tradition. Because her text
differs considerably from the two versions in
Child but is nearly as compelling as either, it is
reprinted here:

137

Oh mourn, oh mourn, ye Lowlands,
    Oh mourn, ye Highlands a'
They have slain the Earl of Murray,
    On the greensward ha' [did?] he fa'.

Oh shame be to ye Huntly,
    To treat your brother sae,
To meet him wi' your claymore,
    And in his bed to slay.

Oh, your lady will be sorrowfu'
    When ye to hame have sped,
An' she learns the Earl of Murray
    You have murdered in his bed.

An' your corn will often ripen,
    And your meadow grass grow green,
Ere you in Dinnybristle town
    Will daurna [daur noo?] to be seen.[30]

This version suggests that many American texts of
the Child ballads may very well be variants of
texts never collected in Britain. In other words,
texts which have travelled for some generations in
America have not in every case been altered as
much as we might expect. Variation must have taken
place before the songs left Scotland, where some
of the American prototypes have never been collected.

    Thus far the Scottish ballad as a new arrival
in America has been illustrated. Similar examples,
having lately travelled from Scotland to America,
appear in various American collections. But none
of the collectors would insist that a first generation ballad be called traditional in America
until such time as it has travelled long enough in
oral circulation to enter popular repertories. All
these emigrant texts are important, however; they
display the kind of ballad diction that was
brought over by Scots and Ulster Scots during the
eighteenth century, when America was in its formative stages and when ballads were popular with a

138

broad section of the population.

After being uprooted and transferred to America, Lowland folk literature could survive if it were of a flexible, translatable nature; that is, if it could compromise with the American diction. In most cases it would be required to suffer many alterations in order to merge with the culturally powerful Anglo-American tradition which surrounded it on all sides. The Scottish ballad, along with numerous Lowland folksongs, was able to take hold in American popular tradition because of its metrical form, its story structure, and its diction: three combined qualities which prevented Gaelic literature, by its nature, from adapting to the American climate.

It is now to the point to discuss the Scottish ballad in its three stages of development — from emigration, to early signs of change, and then to naturalisation. An unpublished but excellent example is 'The Bonnie Hoose of Airlie', which was recorded by Cecil Sharp in New York City from the singing of Mrs Margaret Clapp in 1917. The entire text is presented here to invite comparison between it and the later texts published by other American collectors. Although a few Scottish words colour the diction and help to round out the rhyme, and although the transcription attempts to duplicate the singer's dialect, this version shows tendencies towards naturalisation:

> It fell on a day, a bonny summer day,
> When the leaves were green and yellow,
> That there fell oot a great dispute
> Between Argyle and Airlie.
>
> Argyle he has ta'en a hunder o' his men,
> A hunder men and fifty,
> And he's awa' on yon green strand
> To plunder the bonny house o' Airlie.
>
> The lady looked over the high castle wa',
> And O she sighes sairly

When she saw Argyle and a' his men
Come to plunder the bonny house o' Airlie.

Come doon to me, said proud Argyle,
Come doon to me, Lady Airlie,
Or I swear by the swerd I haud in my hand
I winna' leave a standin' stane in Airlie.

I'll no come doon, ye proud Argyle,
Until that ye speak mair fairly,
Though ye swear by the swerd that ye haud in
  ye're hand
That ye winna' leave a standin' stane in Airlie.

Had my ain lord been at his hame
As he's awa' wi' Charlie,
There's no a Campbell in a' Argyle
Daured hae trod on the bonny green o' Airlie.

But since we can haud oot nae mair,
My hand I offer fairly,
O lead me doon to yonder glen
That I may na' see the burnin' o' Airlie.

He's ta'en her by the trembling hand,
But he's no ta'en her fairly,
For he's led her up to a high hill tap
Where she saw the burnin' o' Airlie.

Clouds o' smoke and flames sae high
Soon left the wa's but barely,
And she lay doon on that hill to die
When she saw the burnin' o' Airlie.[31]

For convenience, the above version of 'The
Bonnie Hoose o' Airlie' can be classified as a
'first generation' or *transitional* Scottish ballad
in America; that is, it shows evidences of transition beyond the emigrant stage. It is neither
standard English nor very convincing Scots in diction, and the pronunciation used by the singer may
have been a wavering between the two.[32] Theoreti-
cally, ballads classified as 'first generation'
are traceable to a Scottish-born parent who sang

the text to his children and grandchildren, and
they in turn exercised a kind of folk-right to
make certain modifications before they were asked
to record the ballad for a collector.

Thereafter, in the third and final stage, the
Scottish diction of the traditional ballads has
become almost completely obliterated in America.
Oral circulation over a period of several generations, 'environmental adjustment', and the over-
powering American speech have all contributed to
the erasure of the original. But traces of the
earlier state can occasionally be detected; a
careful examination of American texts will frequently reveal Scottish characteristics beneath
the surface superimposed by succeeding generations
of singers. What would appear to be an English
ballad in America — on first reading or first
hearing — may sometimes be discerned as clearly
Scottish when the text is submitted to analysis.
Most of the Scottish ballads in America fall into
this third and final classification. This is the
group which has become 'naturalised', the group
that collectors and students are prone to refer to
as English. By and large, these texts are the most
interesting to the analyst.

A case in point is the second version of 'Sir
Patrick Spens' ever recorded in America. It was
sung by Miss Clara J.McCauley of Knoxville, Tennessee, and published in the *Southern Folklore
Quarterly*. Except for place names and the title,
all signs point to complete naturalisation: the
Scottish diction has become anglicised; the *shoon-
aboon* rhyme has been dropped; and the story has
been abbreviated to nine stanzas.

The king sits in Dumferling town,
Adrinking his blood red wine,
'Sir Patrick Spence is the best sailor
That ever sailed the brine.'

The king still sits in Dumferling town,

141

And asipping his red, red wine,
'Now where can I get a good sailor
To man this ship o' mine?'

Oh up then said a yellow haired lad
Just by the king's left knee,
'Sir Patrick Spence is the best skipper
That ever sailed the sea.'

The king he wrote a good letter
And asealed it with his hand;
And when Sir Patrick Spence got it
He was strolling on the sand.

Sir Patrick read the orders from the king
That made him laugh at first,
But as he read another sad line,
Sir Patrick feared the worst.

He took his ship to far Norway,
Asailing o'er the sea,
To get a lovely maiden fair
And to fetch her back, said he.

They sailed and sailed for many a day
Upon the wild, wild sea,
But our good sailor Sir Patrick Spence
Was drowned in the deep.

So the king sits on in Dumferling town
Adrinking his blood red wine,
'Oh, where can I get a good sailor
To sail this ship of mine?'[33]

One of the best preserved of the naturalised
Scottish ballads in America is a text of 'Fair
Annie' (Child 62), which Combs recorded in West
Virginia and published in Part Two of his collection under *Chansons d'Origine Anglaise*.[34] He
failed to note, however, that the text is Scottish
in origin.

The story begins with an Indian incident, which
is perhaps a frontier addition:

(1)

The Indians stole fair Annie
  As she walked by the sea,
But Lord Harry for her a ransom paid,
  In gold and silver money.

(2)

She lived far away with him,
  And none knew whence she came;
She lived in a mansion-house with her love,
  But never told her name.

Next comes the verse which usually introduces the
story in the Scottish versions and which is very
much like Child A (1):

(3)

'Now make your bed all narrow,
  And learn to lie alone:
For I'm going far away, Annie,
  To bring my sweet bride home.'

Child A (1)

'It's narrow, narrow, make your bed,
  And learn to lie your lane;
For I'm ga'n oer the sea, Fair Annie,
  A braw bride to bring hame.
Wi her I will get gowd and gear;
  Wi you I neer got nane.'

This 'extended' stanza of six lines in Child A has
its narrative counterpart in a four-line stanza in
Combs, which adds, incidentally, an American reference to slavery:

(4)

'I'm going far over the river
  To bring my sweet bride home;
For she brings me land and slaves,
  And with you I can get none.'

The question about the new bride's reception by
the patient wife is altered only slightly in
America:

(5)

'But who will spread the wedding feast,
   And pour the red red wine?
And who will welcome my sweet bride,
   My bonny bride so fine?'

Child A (2)

'But wha will bake my bridal bread,
   Or brew my bridal ale?
And wha will welcome my brisk bride,
   That I bring oer the dale?'

The reply by Fair Annie is similar in the American
and Scottish versions:

(6)

'O I will spread the wedding feast,
   And I will pour the red red wine,
And I will welcome your sweet bride,
   Your bonnie bride so fine.'

Child A (3)

'It's I will bake your bridal bread,
   And brew your bridal ale,
And I will welcome your brisk bride,
   That you bring oer the dale.'

The Combs seventh stanza follows the Child version
closely, even to the retention of identical rhyme
words:

(7)

'For she who welcomes my sweet bride
   Must look like a maiden fair,
With lace on her robe so narrow,
   And flowers among her hair.'

144

Child A (4)

'But she that welcomes my brisk bride
  Maun gang like maiden fair;
She maun lace on her robe sae jimp,
  And braid her yellow hair.'

Stanza eight in Combs is not found in any of the
Child versions:

(8)

'Do up, do up your yellow hair,
  And knot it on your neck,
And see you look as maiden-like
  As when I met you first.'

Next follows an American stanza that further illus-
trates the Scottish background of the ballad. The
rhymes are *none* and *again*, which are legitimate
when read in Scots:

(9)

'How can I look so maiden-like,
  When maiden I am *none*?
Have I not had six sons by thee,
  And am with child *again*?

Child A (5)

'But how can I gang maiden-like,
  When maiden I am *nane*?
Have I not born seven sons to thee,
  And am with child *again*?

The next American stanza reveals the same type of
rhyme alteration:

(10)

Four months were past and gone,
  And the word to fair Annie *came*,
That the boat was back from the river,
  With the sweet bonny bride at *home*.
                            [Scottish: *hame*]

145

Other stanzas, chosen at random, reflect
interesting vocabulary substitutions in America:

(20)

'But if my sons were seven rats
    Running over the *milk-house* wall,
And if I were a great gray cat,
    How I would worry them all!'

Child A (23)

'Gin my seven sons were seven young rats,
    Running on the *castle wa'*,
And I were a grey cat mysell,
    I soon would worry them a'.'

Stanza fifteen in Combs is poorly rhymed, for
yours ends both the second and fourth strophes:

(15)

'O welcome home, my fair lady,
    For all that's here is *yours*;
O welcome home, my fair lady,
    And you are safe with *yours*.'

Child I (24)

'You're welcome, you're welcome, fair ladie,
    To your halls but an your *bouers*;
And sae are a' thir gay ladies;
    For a' that's here is *yours*.'

Another faulty rhyme was committed when singers
over several generations dropped the Scottish verb
greet (to weep, cry) for the more usual English
noun *grief*:

(24)

'I'll slip on my dress,' said the new come bride,
    'And draw my shoes over my *feet*;
I will see who so sadly sings,
    And what it is that makes her *grief*.'

The interesting line-for-line changes in the above stanza may be compared to the 'original' in Child:

Child A (26)

'My gown is on,' said the new-come bride,
  'My shoes are on my *feet*,
And I will to Fair Annie's chamber,
  And see what gars her *greet*.'

Furthermore, the West Virginia version retains what appears to be a distinctively Scottish mark in the name of Fair Annie's parents, whose identity she finally reveals (in most versions) at the end of the ballad. The spelling and pronunciation of the surname are altered:

(20)

'The Lord of *Salter* was my father,
  The Lady of *Salter* was my mother;
Young Susan was my dear sister,
  And Lord James was my brother.'

The name originally sung here seems to have been that of the Lord of Saltoun, although it is not the name given in any of the Child versions, and Saltoun (accent on the first syllable) has become the Lord of Salter in America. It is an established title dating to medieval Scotia. But in ballad writings it is best remembered in connection with Andrew Fletcher of Saltoun, the Scottish patriot who fought bitterly the union of the English and Scottish Parliaments in 1707 and who said he cared not who made the laws of the land so long as he could make the ballads.

Of considerable interest is an 'Edward' text from Vermont which Helen H.Flanders recorded and published in *Ballads Migrant in New England*. The ballad diction has become completely anglicised — or Americanised — so much so that a superficial estimate would argue an English origin. Closer examination points again to Scotland:

147

It was in the Mid-Lothian Country,
  Up near the Pentland hills,
Two brothers met one summer's day
  To test their strength and skill.

The place names reveal the origin of this particular version, which the singer remembered as
having come down to him through 'the Douglas
branch' of his family. Some of the rhymes help to
substantiate the claim:

(7)

He raised his brother upon his feet,
  And helped him to the stream so fair.
Frantically he bathed his bloody wounds,
  But they bled more and more. [*mair and mair*][35]

This entire text provides a rewarding study, for
it is an example of how one ballad has acquired
stanzas from others. In this case 'Edward' (Child
13) has borrowed from 'The Twa Brothers' (Child
49) and 'Lizie Wan' (Child 51). All three of these
are Scottish. So did the process of accretion take
place in Scotland before the ballad emigrated? Or
did the Douglas family unconsciously create the
new version after coming to America? Whatever the
case, the constituents are Scottish, and the final
version is convincing on its own merits.

A thorough study of texts and tunes together
will further identify the Scottish element. For
example, in the unabridged Child we find twenty-
six versions of 'Lamkin', including fragments.
Bertrand H.Bronson has included thirty versions in
The Traditional Tunes of the Child Ballads, twenty-
eight of them from North America. In a revealing
headnote Bronson comments:

Miss Annie G.Gilchrist, in a valuable study of
this ballad (JEFDSS, I, No.1, 1932, pp.1-17),
distinguishes between two traditions, the Scot-

tish and the Northumbrian. The Scottish, she believes, has been carried into the Appalachians ...the Scottish tradition favors the gapped scales, and the English the heptatonic.[36]

Now, with both words and music conveniently to hand in Bronson's monumental collection, we can make comparisons with greater confidence than ever before.

Here juxtaposed are selected stanzas from Child B and stanzas from Bronson 5a:

Child B	*Bronson 5a*
(1)	(1)

Balankin was as gude a mason
   as err picked a stane;
He built up Prime Castle,
   but payment gat nane.

Bolakins was a very fine mason
   As ever laid stone.
He built a fine castle
   And the pay he got none.

(5)   (2)

'O where is your good lord?'
   said Lambert Linkin:
'He's awa to New England,
   to meet with his king.'

'Where is the gentleman?
   Is he at home?'
'He's gone to Marion
   For to visit his son.'

(8)   (3)

'O where is your lady?'
   said Lambert Linkin.
'She's in her bower sleeping,'
   said the false nurse to him.

'Where is the lady?
   Is she at home?'
'She's upstairs sleeping,'
   Said the foster to him.

(9)   (4)

'How can I get at her?'
   said Lambert Linkin.
'Stab the babe to the heart,
   wi a silver bokin.'

'How will we get her down
   Such a dark night as this?'
'We'll stick her little baby
   Full of needles and pins.'

(11)   (5)

Balankin he rocked,
   and the false nurse she sang,

The foster she rocked,
   And Bolakins he sung,

Till all the tores of the cradle   While blood and tears
   wi the red blood down ran.   From the cradle did run.

The Bronson verson — from North Carolina, collected by Herbert Halpert in 1939 — shows typical
marks of change and naturalisation in the New
World: *false nurse* becomes *foster*; *tores* becomes
tears; *bokin* (*bodkin*) becomes *needles and pins*.

In many other cases Bronson's extensive
analyses of the tunes, and his references to
probable sources, very often point back to Scotland rather than England. About 'Sir Patrick Spens'
he says: 'The ballad belongs to the Scots alone
and has come to America without English or Irish
assistance.' Squarely in Scottish tradition Bronson puts his second (B) group of tunes for 'Bonny
Barbara Allan'— 'mainly confined to Scotland' but
also sung widely in North America. Of 'Young
Hunting' he wrote: 'This Scottish ballad, if it
ever had any currency in England, seems to have
left no trace there, but to have passed directly
to this country [U.S.A.], where it has enjoyed a
great vogue in our own century — at least in the
Appalachians'. Of 'Bessy Bell and Mary Gray': 'Two
tunes have been preserved, one from Scottish
tradition, the other from Maine, also probably
Scottish.'

Space limitations prevent a survey of the musical evidence. We need only look at each ballad on
the Primary and Secondary lists and consult Bronson in order to see the Scottish nature and af-
filiations of the music collected in America. It
can further be seen that the tunes fall into the
same categories which have been suggested for the
texts: the *emigrant* tune (frequently pentatonic);
the *transitional* (frequently shifting from pentatonic to hexatonic); and finally the *naturalised*
(sometimes heptatonic, sometimes moving from one
of the modes to a standard major scale).

We conclude then, that Scottish ballads and
their tunes emigrated in force to America and pro-

vided the foundation, with other homogeneous
strains, for a strong American tradition. We may
also conclude that at least one third of the so-
called 'British' ballads so far collected in
American oral tradition were originally Scottish,
and that at least nine or ten others are very
possibly a part of the Scottish contribution to
American folksong. Since the 'British' total in
America is slightly more than one hundred, as
listed by Coffin,[37] the Scottish content would
appear to be approximately forty to fifty per cent
of the whole.

Such a brief survey can hardly do justice to
such a distinctive folk legacy. Statistics can
hardly measure the wisdom or aesthetics purveyed
by a strong virile tradition which travelled from
Scotland to America. For now, we can only point to
and identify in the New World an ancient, ageless,
and at times heroic contribution of song and story.

λ

8. WHEN IS A POEM LIKE A SUNSET?

J.M.Sinclair

WHEN IS A poem like a sunset? The short answer is:
when it is composed in an oral tradition. We normally discuss the appreciation of natural phenom-
ena, like sunsets, in different terms from artefacts, like poems. It is no longer usual for
people to look for the same sort of meaning in
sunsets as they expect in language. If they did,
they would be investing sunsets with the qualities
of tastefully-presented omens.

Natural language is subject to natural laws,
and several sets of these natural laws concern
changes due to the passage of time. In the first
place, a text itself may be damaged or destroyed,
as may any artefact. Here literature is in a
favourable position as compared to paintings,
sculpture, architecture, etc.; for while a particular copy of a text may be at risk, a language
text may be copied endlessly or remembered and
passed orally for a time. A text, like a musical
score, is almost independent of physical objects.

Secondly, an artefact is composed within a certain
specific culture, and depends on convevtions of that
culture for part of its meaning. The conventions
change with time, and although the physical appearance of the artefact may survive intact, its meaning may change. The special meaning of words in a
poetic diction, the significance of a halo in
religious paintings, may be difficult to recapture.

There is a third area of change which is particularly hazardous for a literary text, but which
is irrelevant to other artefacts. A painting may
have world-wide appeal even though the paint has
faded, even though most of its admirers are not
keenly conscious of the conventions surrounding
its composition. A literary text has meaning only
by comparison with a particular language at a particular time. Any stretch of language has meaning only

153

as a sample of an enormously large body of text; it represents the results of a complicated selection process, and each selection has meaning by virtue of all the other selections which might have been made, but have been rejected. By studying a very long text, or by interrogating a native speaker, some approximation to the total set of selections, and their priorities, etc., may be set out, and the description so produced may be used in order to talk about the meaning of a shorter text.

So a poem is a sample of a language; perhaps not a representative sample, but only carrying meaning because it can be referred to a description of a whole language. We assume that an educated native speaker, contemporary to the poem, has such a description built in, and may be said to have the potentiality of understanding the poem; anyone else must be taught.

A great deal is known about the language used in earlier periods in English-speaking areas. When this knowledge is applied to the literature, some account can be given of, say, the meaning of a Shakespeare play to its original audience.[1] There does not seem to be as much help available on the *judgement* of gains and losses in meaning through changes in time.[2] Although the text stays the same, the language, its reference-framework, changes; therefore its effect on a reader changes and the basis of his judgements becomes worthy of careful inspection. Whatever the theoretical objections to having our cake and eating it, in practice we may find such an attitude difficult to avoid. We go to a performance of a Shakespeare play conscious of having to make allowances; changes in the language may have made a serious line sound very funny, and we are on the alert to avoid laughing, and to adjust our reactions according to the extent of our knowledge of the period. In short, we tolerate. Rarely is there any balancing adjustment to devalue the happy accidents that may have befallen the meaning of the text.

Appreciation and evaluation become more tricky still when we consider the operation of natural laws during the actual composition of works of literature, as happens in an oral tradition. Lines imperfectly remembered, lines meaningless to the performer being jumbled, phrases consciously archaised, etc. It must be assumed that such factors are present in the actual composition of a work which comes to us through an oral tradition. They are as likely to have been the origin of a fine phrase or an obscurity as is the creative mind of an author in a written tradition, whose original text is usually discoverable. Although such an author may have been affected during composition by all sorts of random occurrences, there is a great difference between a text for which an author accepts responsibility and one which has been seriously affected by natural laws, long after its original composer relinquished responsibility for it.

Where there are several extant versions of a text composed in an oral tradition, some hints may be gained about the effect of the handing-down process. But rarely is there anything approximating to a complete record of the textual history; rarely can one be sure that a set of texts represents a continuous sequence without any branching. There is usually a danger of stylistic evidence being used in the placing of texts relative to each other, and in that event the set of texts cannot yield stylistic information without circularity.

In view of the inadequacies of the surviving texts, I decided some years ago to manufacture my own texts. I set up a brief 'oral tradition' and passed a text down to see what would happen to it. The first experiment, which I will describe in this paper, was purely preliminary. I wanted the

results of it to suggest the lines on which a more
scientific experiment could be carried out. However, despite its informal setting, the experiment
revealed features which are of immediate interest
both in my present subject and in more general
considerations of how literary texts give meaning.

First, a few words about the circumstances of
the experiment. Six of my students agreed to take
part,[3] and one of them learned by heart a chosen
version of Keats's 'La Belle Dame Sans Merci'.
From that point on, none of the participants consulted a text of the poem. Allowing at least a
week to elapse, the first student passed the poem
orally to the next by reciting it over and over
again until the two agreed that the poem had been
accurately transmitted. Then, and only then, the
first participant wrote out the version just
transmitted and gave it to me. In due course I
collected six versions of the poem, representing
its progress down the line.

This synthetic oral tradition is open to any
number of criticisms concerning how accurately it
simulates a real one. University students were
used, the poem was already familiar to them, the
time element was ridiculously compressed, etc.
Nevertheless, it remains very likely that the
changes discussed below are at least of the same
general type as the actual changes which have
affected extant ballad poetry.

Now to the presentation of the changes themselves. I propose to tabulate these initially according to the position of altered syllables in
the rhythm and grammar of the poem. Then I will
tentatively classify them according to my assess-
ment of their stylistic effect, of the way they
have altered the meaning of the poem. To show the
total effect of the changes, the poem is printed
in square brackets above a 'composite change version'. Some of the changes were lost in the final
version, because the original readings were re-

stored; so I have put together a text which shows
as many of the changes as is possible in a single
version.

1 [Ah what can ail thee wretched wight
   Alone and palely loitering;
   The sedge is withered from the lake,
   And no birds sing.]

1 O what can ail thee wretched knight
   So pale and lonely wandering
   The sedge has withered on the lake
   And no birds sing.

5 [Ah what can ail thee, wretched wight,
   So haggard and so woebegone
   The squirrel's granary is full
   And the harvest's done.]

5 O what can ail thee wretched knight
   So pale and lonely wandering
   The squirrel's granary is full
   And no birds sing.

9 [I see a lily on thy brow
   With anguish moist and fever dew
   And on thy cheek a fading rose
   Fast withereth too.]

9 A lily sits upon thy brow
   Of fever moist and passion dew
   And on thy cheek a fading rose
   Fast withereth too.

13 [I met a lady in the meads
   Full beautiful, a faery's child.
   Her hair was long, her foot was light
   And her eyes were wild.]

13 I saw a lady in the mead
    Full beautiful, a fairy child
    Her hair was long, her foot was light
    And her eye was bright

17 [I set her on my pacing steed
And nothing else saw all day long
For sideways would she lean, and sing
A faery's song.]

17 I took her on my pacing steed
And all day long did ride
She sang a fairy song
And gazed from side to side

21 [I made a garland for her head
And bracelets too and fragrant zone.
She looked at me as she did love
And made sweet moan.]

21 I wove her garlands for her hair
And bracelets sweet, of fragrant zone
And she did look as she did love
And made sweet moan.

25 [She found me roots of relish sweet
And honey wild and manna dew
And sure in language strange she said
I love thee true.]

25 She fetched me roots of relish sweet
And honey wild, and manna dew
She looked at me and sighed
I love you true

29 [She took me to her elfin grot
And there she gazed and sighed deep
And there I shut her wild sad eyes
So kissed to sleep.]

29 She took me to her elfin grot
And there she sighed both long and deep
And there I closed her wild sad eyes
So kissed asleep

33 [And there we slumbered on the moss
And there I dreamed, ah! woe betide!

158

        The latest dream I ever dreamed
        On the cold hill side.]

33 And there we slumbered on the moss
    And there I dreamed, o woe betide
    The latest dream I ever dreamed
    On the cold hillside

37 [I saw pale kings and princes too
     Pale warriors, death-pale were they all
     Who cried La belle dame sans merci
     Hath thee in thrall.]

37 I saw pale kings and princes too
    And warriors pale (death-pale were they all)
    They said La belle dame sans merci
    Has thee enthralled

41 [I saw their starved lips in the gloam
     With horrid warning gaped wide
     And I awoke and found me here
     On the cold hill side.]

41 Their lips were horrid in the gloam
    Horrid warnings gapeth wide
    And then I woke and found myself
    On the cold hillside

45 [And this is why I sojourn here
     Alone and palely loitering
     Though the sedge is withered from the lake
     And no birds sing.]

45 And that is why you see me here
    So pale and lonely wandering
    Tho' sedge has withered on the lake
    And no birds sing.

TABULATION OF CHANGES

Line references are throughout to the original
version. Because certain passages underwent
several changes, the bracketed form in the tables

is not always that of the original, but sometimes of an intermediate reading.

Here and there, especially in the written representation of unstressed syllables, the conventions of writing force one to be more specific than is necessary in speech; several of the changes below may represent a changing interpretation of a constant sound. These are marked with an asterisk.

I have also marked with a sword (†) two changes which happen to restore a rejected draft version of the poet.

A. *Unstressed Syllables*

i Substitution: monosyllabic words

Line 1, 5, 34 :	ah	> o(h)
3*:	is	> has
3, 47 :	from	> on
10 :	with	> of
16 :	were	> was [see also A iii]
21*:	a	> her [see also A iii]
22 :	and	> of > a [syllable no.5]
28 :	thee	> you
39†:	who	> they
40 :	hath	> has
41*:	their	> the
42 :	with	> their > the

ii Changes in word division

2, 6, 46 :	a-	> so [see also C i]
30 :	sighed	> sighed *both* [see also D i]
32*:	to	> a-
40*:	in	> en-
43 :	a-	> then [see also D i]

iii Inflectional changes

8 :	harvest's	> harvest
13 :	meads	> mead
14, 20 :	faery's	> fairy
16 :	eyes	> eye
21 :	garland	> garlands

160

40 : enthrall > enthralled
42 : gaped > gapeth

   iv Rhythm changes
 8 : the (syllable 2) (drops out)
38 : and (is added initially) [see also
       C ii]
42 : with (drops out)
47 : the (syllable 2) (drops out)

B. Stressed Syllables

    1, 5 : wight   > knight
2, 6, 46 : loitering > wandering
      10 : anguish   > passion [see also C i]
      13 : met   > saw
      16 : wild   > bright [see also E ii]
      21 : made   > wove
           head   > hair
      22 : too   > sweet
      25 : found   > fetched > gave
      27 : said   > sighed [see also D ii]
      31 : shut   > closed > shut > closed
      39 : cried   > said
      45 : this   > that

C. Sequence of Words

         i Rhythm preserved
2, 6, 46 : alone and palely > so pale and
           lonely
      10 :   ⎡anguish⎤   ⎡fever ⎤
         :   │fever │   │anguish│
         : with   │anguish│ moist and   │fever │ dew
         :   │passion│   │fever │
         :   ⎣fever ⎦   ⎣passion⎦
      27 : in language strange she said > she
           said in language strange
     40† : hath thee > thee hath

         ii Rhythm altered
      19 : for sideways would she lean > for

161

she would sideways lean [see
also E iii]
38 : pale warriors > warriors pale

D. Rewriting

i Rhythm preserved

30 : gazed and sighed > sighed long and
43 : and I awoke   > and then I woke
45 : I sojourn here   > you see me here

ii Rhythm altered

9 : I see a lily on > a lily sits upon
23 : she looked at me > and she did look
27 : she said in language strange > she
looked at me and said
38 : pale warriors > warriors pale
41 : I saw their starved lips > their
lips were horrid
43 : me here > myself

E. Stanzaic Changes

i Line re-arrangements

6 : replaced by modified line 2
8 : replaced by line 4, line 8 restored
and again replaced by 4.

ii Rhyming

Stanza 4 : a b c b > a b c c

iii Extensive modifications
Stanza 5

The changes range in size from the hardly noticeable alterations in unstressed syllables to
the recasting of a whole stanza. Each of them
changes the meaning of the poem. The next task is
to set up suitable categories in which changes can
be grouped together which seem to cause the same
sort of change in meaning.
    One general category that will be needed is

analogy; the tendency towards regularity. Changes
due to analogy will be those for which there is a
model nearby in the text. The line re-arrangements
in stanza 2 are by analogy with stanza 1, while
the curious change in rhyme-scheme in line 16 is
no doubt due to the occurrence of the rhyming
vowel in line 15 as well as line 14. The following
grammatical changes seem to be based on analogy:

line	*change*	*model*	*line*
2	alone > so pale	so haggard	6
16	her eyes were wild >		
	her eye was wild	her hair was long	
		her foot was light	15
21	I made a garland >		
	I made her garlands	and bracelets	22
23	she looked at me >		
	and she did look	as she did love	23
27	in language strange		
	she said > she looked		
	at me and said	she looked at me as	23
45	I sojourn here >		
	you see me here	and found me here	43

The interesting alteration to line 9 (I see a
lily on thy brow > a lily sits upon thy brow) may
partly be explained as an extension of the kind of
subject found in the first two stanzas. *The sedge,
no birds, squirrel's granary, the harvest* are very
different from the personal pronoun *I* that follows
them. For the rest of the poem, the pronouns *I* and
she are almost the only subjects of clauses. The
point of interest here is that the alteration
causes the subject-change to coincide with the
change of speaker, between stanzas 3 and 4. In the
original version, the first *I* in line 9 refers to
the questioner, and all subsequent ones to the
wight himself. The altered version simplifies the
structure of the poem as a whole.

In the vast majority of the changes, the rhythm
is left alone or altered only slightly. Line 47 is

almost identical to line 3, and it loses a syllable which makes it rhythmically identical. Line 8 also loses a syllable, perhaps because of the influence of line 4.

Twice in the poem word-substitutions echo nearby words. Both these changes are further discussed later on, but may be mentioned here.

Line 41 : starved > horrid : *model* : horrid 42
27 : said > sighed : *model* : sighed 30

The next general stylistic category that it is profitable to set up is *revision*. By this I mean both the modernising of archaic forms and the replacement of poetic structures by structures more common in non-literary modern English. In several places the participants have replaced words and phrases which were not very familiar to them by approximately equivalent words and phrases in their everyday idiom. The examples below show that 'equivalence' may mean many things.

In line 3 *is withered* becomes *has withered*, and again in line 47. The older form of the 'perfect' tense is rejected. Other verbal points concern the change from *hath* to *has* (line 40) and the loss of the second syllable in *sighed* (30). Oddly enough, the other verb which has one more syllable in the poem than it has in modern English changes into an archaic form, *gaped* > *gapeth*, line 42. Among the pronouns, *thee* becomes *you* (28) and *this* (45) becomes the much more natural *that*. A neat change in line 43, *and found me here* > *and found myself* inserts, correctly for Modern English, the reflexive pronoun. Two adverbial elements are reduced in prominence by being shifted nearer to their most usual positions of occurrence (lines 19 and 27).

Several vocabulary changes can be assigned to this category. The word *thrall* (40) by various changes becomes the common enough word *enthralled*, but with quite a change in meaning! Line 43 has a vocabulary change involving slight modernisation:

and I awoke > and then I woke

but also the introduction of *then* could be seen as
a grammatical revision. *Loitering* probably is
picking up taboo associations; for a while it is
replaced by *wandering* (lines 2, 46). *Wight* (1, 5)
becomes *knight*, almost certainly influenced by an
alternative version of the poem (O what can ail
thee, Knight at arms): and *sojourn* (45) gets a
face-lift: *I sojourn here* > *you see me here*.

These are the main indications of *revision*. But
I want to include in this category those changes
which seem to involve misunderstanding of, or
failure to understand, the meaning of a passage.
In one way or another, the changes we have mentioned so far have been restrained by considerations of rhythm and meaning. Once the original
meaning ceases to be an important factor, one can
expect fairly radical changes. Line 10 offers a
fine example. If I understand Keats correctly,
what he wrote is roughly paraphrasable as 'moist
with anguish and the dew produced by a fever'. The
tortuous syntax of line 10 fights against the
structural parallelism of *anguish moist* and *fever
dew*. The two phrases have the same syllabification,
the same position in the half-line, and their
meanings are very similar. *Anguish* and *fever* are
both nouns; in fact there is only one clear
pointer to the underlying syntax: that *dew* is not
normally an adjective. My participants made it an
adjective, and, having lost the sense, permutated
the nouns with gusto (see C i above). The change
in the initial syllable of the line, *with* > *of*,
underlines the loss of the syntactic meaning;
moist of anguish is an impossible construction in
modern English.

The alterations to line 22 reflect what is perhaps a minor obscurity in the poem. Keats wrote
'And bracelets too, and fragrant zone'. It would
seem that the speaker made circlets for the lady's

head, wrists and waist. But if so the line would
be more likely to read *and fragrant zones*, or *and
a fragrant zone*. But as it stands, a 'mass' noun
is an archaic meaning and an odd construction: it
is ripe for alteration. *Of fragrant zone* — presumably zone is a flower. *A fragrant zone* — here we
have a nominal expression in a vaguely appositional relationship to what precedes it.

It might be a little uncharitable to place the
change in line 41 in this category: *I saw their
starved lips* > *their lips were horrid*. The meaning of *starve*, perhaps, is misunderstood. In fact
this line is one of six together (37-42) where so
many changes occur that one is led to the conclusion that the narrative was found difficult to
follow there. The appositional group *pale warriors*
in 38 becomes linked to the preceding line by *and*,
and eventually drops the *pale*. Other examples tend
to dislocate the syntax. The relative clause *who
cried* becomes a second main clause *they cried*; the
clear reference of *their* in *their starved lips*
(41) becomes ambiguous when *their* changes to *the*;
the loss of the initial preposition *with* in line
42 causes the subject of *gaped* to change from
their starved lips to *horrid warnings*. The dropped
initial syllable in this line returns as *their*,
and eventually *the*. Keats contrived a subtle mixture of the open-mouthed warning and the fixed
gape of a dead face. Our resultant version was
very close to nonsense.

It may be significant that in lines 38 and 40
occur two of the very few instances of a pattern
running counter to revision, the tendency to
archaise and poeticise. If the narrative thread
has been lost, the spirit of the passage, at least,
has been preserved.

I shall call the third and last category *approximation*. In this category will come alterations which seem to have arisen largely through
forgetfulness of detail. A word perhaps is re-

placed by one similar in meaning, but not by
analogy and without the implications of revision.
As one might expect, Section B of the tabulation
(stressed-syllable changes) provides a number of
the examples:

13 I *met* a lady	>	*saw*
21 I *made* her garlands for her *head*	>	*wove...hair*
22 and bracelets *too*	>	*sweet*
25 she *found* me roots	>	*fetched* > *gave*
27 in language strange she *said*	>	*sighed*
30 she *gazed and sighed* deep	>	*sighed long and*
31 I *shut* her wild sad eyes	>	*closed* > *shut* > *closed*
39 who *cried* La belle dame	>	*said*

The easy alternation in line 31 points towards
synonymity; other changes may be considered as
substitutions of vocabulary items with similar
meanings but different *ranges*. *Found* has a wider
range of potential occurrence than *fetched*, but
gave is the widest of the three. *Said* narrows to
sighed but *cried* widens to *said*. There is no evidence of a 'watering down' of the poetic effects
in this area, since many of the changes represent
something more like a 'concentration' of meaning.

The change in line 22 is more drastic than most
and requires a slight digression, because it may
partly be due to analogy. The second lines of
stanzas in the poem frequently contain parallel
structures (certainly stanzas 2, 3, 7, 8 and 10)
Bracelets sweet creates a chiastic pattern with
fragrant zone, whereas *bracelets too* does not.
Further, the structure of 'noun + adjective' is
virtually extinct in modern English, and it is one
of the most obvious poetic archaisms in this poem.
In the same stanzaic position as *bracelets sweet*
occur *anguish moist* and *honey wild*; later on in the
poem, *pale warriors* becomes *warriors pale* in the

same stanzaic position. These facts are hints of analogy working over a greater extent of text than we have allowed for.

To return to the examples of approximation. A few of the inflexional changes (see Section A iii) are of this type.

	8 and the *harvest's done*	>	*harvest*
	13 in the *meads*	>	*mead*
14, 20	a *faery's* child	>	*fairy*
	a *faery's* song		
	14 with horrid *warning*	>	*warnings*

These are minor alterations in syntax. That in line 8 complicates the syntax because the new version presupposes the *is* of line 7.

The tiny changes in lines 3 and 47 merit attention, to show the sort of effect an approximation can have on the meaning of a line:

the sedge *is* withered *from* the lake > *has...on*

Keats wrote a rather subtle line which combined two distinct meanings. The line might be paraphrased as:

'The sedge on the lake is withered, and, being withered, gives the impression of having disappeared from the lake.'

The conflated meaning is achieved by two devices:
a the ambiguity in *is*, already mentioned on page 164,
b the selection of *from*, which is an odd preposition to use alongside the verb *wither*.
The altered version flattens out the meaning by firmly selecting one of the alternatives.

The three categories are sufficient for all but a handful of the changes in the poem; *analogy*, the influence of the immediate language environment; *revision*, the influence of the modern speaker's habits of language; and *approximation*, the influence of his inexact memory for detail. I hope this

paper has shown the power they have to transform
a text so much that its own author would hardly
recognise it. All three categories may be assumed
to have played a part in the actual composition of
works that were passed down in an oral tradition.
How then do we assess the obscurities, clichés,
simple structures, parallelisms, non sequiturs,
refrains, etc., of our heritage of oral poetry? As
poems, or at least, in part, as sunsets?

NOTES

1. *Popular Ballad and Medieval Romance*

Holger Olof Nygard

[1] Notably in D.K.Wilgus, *Anglo-American Folksong Scholarship since 1898* (New Brunswick, N.J., 1959), Chapters 1 and 2.

[2] *The Ballad of Tradition* (Oxford, 1932), p.59.

[3] *Ibid.*, p.189.

[4] Andrew Lang, in his article 'Ballads' in the *Encyclopaedia Britannica*, 11th ed., in praising Child for his wisdom in the matter, refers to the headnote to *Young Beichan* (53) as an example. The *Young Beichan* ballad, however, has not drawn from Child a mention of this particular problem of sources. Lang very probably had the *Sir Aldingar* headnote in mind.

As Thelma James, in her article 'The English and Scottish Popular Ballads and Francis J.Child', *Journal of American Folklore*, XLVI (1933), 51-68, has demonstrated, Professor Child's views concerning the nature of the popular ballad did undergo considerable change from the time of his first collection in 1857 to the publication of the major edition. The first collection contains a number of romance-like pieces that he later laid aside when he edited his 1882-98 collection. *The English and Scottish Ballads* of 1857 was markedly in the tradition of Bishop Percy's *Reliques*, in which popular ballad and romance appeared side by side as cullings of ancient poetry.

[5] Paul Christopherson has attempted to untie and sort out, with less circumspection and uncertain results, the far-reaching strands of the tale to be found in *Sir Aldingar*, in his *Ballad of 'Sir*

Aldingar': Its Origins and Analogues (Oxford, 1952).

6 *English and Scottish Popular Ballads*, 5 vols. (Boston, 1882-98), II, 43-44.

7 *Ibid.*, p.44n.

8 *Op.cit.*, I, 96.

9 *Ibid.*, II, 67.

10 'Professor Child and the Ballad', *PMLA*, XXI (1906), 758.

11 'Ballad Poetry'. *Johnson's Universal Cyclopaedia* (New York, 1896), I, 464.

12 See T.F.Henderson, *The Ballad in Literature* (Cambridge, 1912), p.95.

13 *Op.cit.*, I, 257.

14 Cited in Henderson, *op.cit.*, p.80.

15 Page xxv.

16 Kittredge's summation of the communal theory and denial of romance origins for the ballad begins on p.xxvii of his Introduction; his closing of the troublesome chapter occurs on p.xxx.

17 (Boston), p.lxxi.

18 (Boston), p.68.

19 Cited in L.C.Wimberly, *Folklore in the English and Scottish Ballads* (Chicago, 1928), p.13.

20 *Op.cit.*, I, 188.

21 *The Popular Ballad*, p.216.

22 *Ibid.*, p.231. Gummere is here quoting Child, II, 61.

23 *Loc.cit.*

24 *Ibid.*, p.232.

25 *History of English Poetry*, 5 vols. (New York, 1895), I, 445.

26 *Ibid.*, pp.445-446.

27 *Loc.cit.*

28 Page 186. See his 'Ballads' article in the *Encyclopaedia Britannica*, 14th ed., for a systematic attack upon the communalists and a defence of the romance origin theory.

29 *Op.cit.*, p.65.

30 *Ibid.*, p.96.

31 2nd ed. (Edinburgh, 1910), p.359.

32 (New York), p.190.

33 *Ibid.*, p.187.

34 *Ibid.*, p.189.

35 Cited in Henderson, *Scottish Vernacular Literature*, p.345.

36 'The Mystery of "The Queen's Marie"',*Blackwood's Magazine*, 158 (1895), 381.

37 Cited in Wimberly, *op.cit.*, p.15.

38 'On the History of the Ballads, 1100-1500', *Proceedings of the British Academy, 1909-10* (London, 1910), p.203.

39 *Ibid.*, p.200.

40 *Ibid.*, p.199.

41 *The Transition Period*, p.180.

42 *Cambridge History of English Literature*, II, 470.

43 C.S.Baldwin, cited in Wimberly, *op.cit.*, p.14.

44 *The Medieval Popular Ballad*, trans. E.G.Cox
   (Boston, 1914), p.193.

45 *Op.cit.*, p.204.

46 Child has occasion to mention about seventy-
   five romances and romance associated works,
   ranging from Ovid's *Metamorphoses* and the *Gesta
   Romanorum* to Spenser's *Faerie Queene*. These
   references to romances occur in the headnotes
   to sixty-three separate ballads. His intent in
   the greater number of cases it to point out a
   similarity of theme or motif rather than an
   actual indebtedness of one form to the other.

47 *English Literature at the Close of the Middle
   Ages* (Oxford, 1945), p.184.

2. *THE WEE WEE MAN* AND *ALS Y YOD ON AY MOUNDAY*

   E.B.Lyle

1 It is printed with the title *A ballad on the
   Scotish wars* in the revised edition of Ritson's
   Ancient Songs and Ballads (London, 1829), I.
   40-50. It had previously been printed entire by
   John Finlay in *Scottish Historical and Romantic
   Ballads* (Edinburgh, 1808), II. 163-205, and
   Thomas Warton had included lines 1-12, 17-22,
   35-8 and 69-72 of the introductory narrative in
   a note in *The History of English Poetry* III
   (London, 1781), p.149.

2 BM Cotton Julius A.5, ff. 180r-181v. See John
   Edwin Wells *A Manual of the Writings in Middle
   English 1050-1400* (New Haven and London, 1916),
   pp.222-3, and Rupert Taylor, *The Political
   Prophecy in England* (Columbia University
   Studies in English, New York, 1911), pp.65-7.
   I am extremely grateful to T.M.Smallwood for

his comments on the dating. He tells me that
the text is certainly not earlier than 1307,
the year reached by Langtoft's *Chronicle* which
occurs before it in the manuscript without
manuscript break, and that palaeographically it
can be placed in the first half of the fourteenth century with the second quarter more
probable than the first.

3 Francis James Child, *The English and Scottish
Popular Ballads* (Boston, 1882-98), I.330-3.

4 The texts in group 1 have identical or similar
wording at some or all of the following points:
1.1 As I was walking all alone, 2.3 Span, 5.3
to bait our horse, 6.1 at her Back, 8.2 jimp
and sma. The texts in group 2 do not have any
of the above readings and share the following
points which are not found in the first group:
1.1 As I went forth to take a walk / As I gaed
out to tak a walk, 2.1 thick and short, 4.4 An
ye dinna trow me / Gin ye dinna believe, 5.4
Dame / dame, 6.1 waiting on her / wating on her,
8.3 e'er ye cd a' said what's that / before ye
coud hae sadd what was that.

5 The manuscript containing this collection of
songs made by Elizabeth St Clair has been known
also as the Mansfield manuscript. The variant
of *The Wee Wee Man* is quoted from Frank Miller,
'The Mansfield Manuscript', *Transactions and
Journal of Proceedings of the Dumfriesshire and
Galloway Natural History and Antiquarian
Society* ser. 3, vol. 19 (1933-35), pp.83-4.

6 David Herd, *Ancient and Modern Scottish Songs*
(2nd edition, Edinburgh, 1776). The text quoted
is that of James Kinsley in *The Oxford Book of
Ballads* (Oxford, 1969), pp.11-12, which is
taken from the Herd MS (BM Add.22311), p.153.

[7] The text is quoted from Child, I.333-4. The word 'sothe' in line 5 is given by him in square brackets as a conjectural addition.

[8] *The Oxford Book of Medieval English Verse* ed. Celia and Kenneth Sisam (Oxford, 1970), p.418.

[9] See further, E.B.Lyle, 'The Relationship between *Thomas the Rhymer* and *Thomas of Erceldoune*', *Leeds Studies in English* N.S. 4 (1970), pp.23-30.

[10] For the seventeenth-century printed text of *Thomas of Erceldoune*, see William P.Albrecht, *The Loathly Lady in 'Thomas of Erceldoune'* (University of New Mexico Publications in Language and Literature No 11, Albuquerque, 1954).

3. HISTORY AND HARLAW

David Buchan

[1] *The English and Scottish Popular Ballads*, III (Boston, 1888), 317. All subsequent allusions to Child's versions of, or comments on, 'Harlaw' refer to III, 316-320.

[2] *Last Leaves of Traditional Ballads and Ballad Airs* (Aberdeen, 1925), p.102. For more versions see Bertrand H.Bronson, *The Traditional Tunes of the Child Ballads* (Princeton, N.J., 1959-72), II, 117-26, IV, 494. The archives of the School of Scottish Studies contain versions by Jeannie Robertson, Norman Kennedy, Robin Hutchison, John Strachan, M.Douglas Gordon, and Lucy Stewart.

[3] W.C.Dickinson, G.Donaldson, and I.A.Milne, *A Source Book of Scottish History*, I (Edinburgh, 1958), 168-170; W.C.Dickinson, *From the Earli-*

est Times to 1603, A New History of Scotland,
I (London, 1961), 202-203.

4 (Aberdeen, 1949), pp.49-53. Two recent historians, Dickinson, p.202, and Fenton Wyness, *City
by the Grey North Sea: Aberdeen* (Aberdeen,
1965), p.129, state, though without indicating
their sources, that the Forbeses took part in
the battle.

5 M.M.Gray, ed., *Scottish Poetry from Barbour to
James VI* (London, 1935), p.243.

6 For relations between the Northeast and the
Highlands see William Watt, *A History of Aberdeen and Banff* (Edinburgh, 1900); James Allar-
dyce, ed., *Papers Relating to the Jacobite
Period 1699-1750*, 2 vols. (Aberdeen, 1895-96);
and the relevant parish accounts in Sir John
Sinclair, ed., *The Statistical Account of Scotland*, 21 vols. (Edinburgh, 1791-97), and
J.Gordon, ed., *New Statistical Account of Scotland*, 18 vols. (Edinburgh, 1843). One coincid-
ental factor which could have facilitated the
ballad's shift in historical focus was the
association in the popular mind of the Forbeses
with the established government; from 1715 to
1745 the foremost adherent of the Hanoverian
house in the North of Scotland was a Forbes,
Duncan Forbes of Culloden.

7 III, 424-428; Simpson, pp.145-146; Greig, pp.
110-112.

4. *THE GREY SELKIE*

Alan Bruford

1 Francis J.Child, *The English and Scottish Popular Ballads*, vol.2, part 4 (Boston, 1886),p.494.

2 A selkie is simply a seal, though readers of
the ballad have tended to assume that in itself
it means a seal which can take human form.
Hence 'The Silkie' has been used not only for
the name of a group of singers, but for a
science fiction novel.

3 F.W.L.Thomas, 'Shetland Ballad', *Proceedings of
the Society of Antiquaries of Scotland* 1 (1852)
86-9. Child gives Thomas's text unchanged,
apart from punctuation and apostrophes, with
the exception of 'quhen' in verse 6, which is
probably not an archaism but an attempt to express a sound which in Shetland varies between
wh and *qu*. 'Schot' and 'schoot' in verse 7 may
also be intended phonetically, perhaps just for
the sonorous Shetland back *sh*. Despite Thomas's
punctuation, verse 6 is obviously spoken by the
father.

4 Karl Blind, 'Scottish, Shetlandic and Germanic
Water Tales, Part II', *The Contemporary Review*
40 (1881) 399-423.

5 Bertrand H.Bronson, *The Traditional Tunes of
the Child Ballads*, Vol.2 (Princeton, N.J.,
1962), pp.564-5.

6 Otto Andersson, 'Väinämöinen och Vellamos
jungfru', *Budkavlen* 26 (1974), 97-132 and
'Ballad hunting in the Orkney Islands', *Budkavlen* 33 (1954) 23-58.

7 The second edition, called *Rambles in the Far
North*, was printed at Paisley in 1884.

8 SA 1970/229 A5, with some minor variants from a
later recording, SA 1972/168 A5 (School of Scottish Studies Archive, University of Edinburgh).

9 'Go wed thu's weds' in both verses 7 and 10 on
the later recording: perhaps Mrs Henderson sang

'Thou may go' as in D.

10 'Pocket' in the later recording: compare E 20
below.

11 Possibly 'a gay gold chain'— is this a remi-
niscence of 'a gey good gold chain'? On the
later recording Mr Henderson said 'a gold ring
upon his hand' (verse 12) and '...on his
flipper' (in the narration), but this is no
doubt merely a slip. Apparently the mother
supplies the chain, as in E but not in D where
the chain seems a substitute for the rejected
ring, and so this verse, not the prophecy,
follows verse 10.

12 In 1972 he also mentioned the late William
Sinclair ('Billy o Stane'), a well-known singer
in the South Parish of South Ronaldsay, as a
source, but he has not repeated this, and
though James Henderson and his cousin John Dass
learned many songs from Billy, this was not one
of them.

13 Verse 1, SA 1972/166 A7; verses 2 and 3, SA
1973/77 B7. Note that the selkie's Dutch-
sounding name is clearly 'Miller' stressed on
the last syllable here. There are several
parallels for the difference in tunes within
one island: thus John Halcro and his second
cousin John Dass have quite distinct tunes for
the shipwreck songs 'The *Middlesex Flora*' and
'The Brig *Columbus*' (of which the first is from
Ireland and the second a local composition).
Though the old Scots lulling syllables 'ba loo
(lillie)' are here assimilated to 'Alleluia'
they are not long out of use: James Henderson's
mother used them so often as a lullaby (to hymn
tunes or any tune that came to mind in her old
age) that his children called her 'Granny Baloo'

14 Vol.8 (1894) 53-8.

15 William Montgomerie, 'The Orkney Play of the
    Lady Odivere in Lowland Scots' and commentary,
    Scots (Burns) Chronicle (1951) 38-61.

16 He even writes in a pamphlet on 'Orkney Wedd-
    ings' (reprinted in *Orkney Folklore and Tradi-
    tions*, ed. Ernest W.Marwick, Kirkwall, 1961,
    p.83): 'The writer thinks that the name came to
    Orkney from Germany.' *Minne* of course means
    'love'. The *Scottish National Dictionary* does
    quote some nineteenth-century and later in-
    stances of *menyie* in the sense of 'throng' or
    'medley' from the North of Scotland, though the
    only Orcadian instances are Dennison's own com-
    pounds *menye-singers* and *menye-cogs*. His spell-
    ing is that commonly used by Scott and other
    historical novelists, and they may be the real
    source.

17 'The ballad was always divided into fits, but I
    have been told that its divisions were once
    called by another name, which I have been un-
    able to discover' (*The Scottish Antiquary* 8.53).
    It seems, however, that 'fit' (a romantic
    archaism) is claimed to be the current name.

18 There are items by Dennison headed 'Orkney Folk-
    lore: Sea Myths' in *The Scottish Antiquary* 5
    (1891) 68-71, 130-3, 167-71; 6 (1892) 115-21;
    and 7 (1893) 18-34, 81-2, 112-20, 171-7. This
    and the following quotation are at 7.23 and
    81-2.

19 *Tocher* 8 (1972) 256-7.

20 'Probably most of the oral verse in Orkney
    would be lost when the Norse language was for-
    gotten by the people; and the fragments that
    remained in the newly adopted language must

have been rude translations by native bards or
menye-singers. While it is therefore unlikely
that we should meet with anything very old in
our oral verse, yet it should not be forgotten
that the Norse and the Scots languages existed
together for a considerable time in these
islands; and to a considerable extent the two
languages became amalgamated. So that the dialect used by the peasantry during the eighteenth century may be regarded as Scoto-Norse,
gradually fading into oblivion before the English of the elementary schools. Without dwelling on the subject, it may be said, that every
word in the ballad added by me has been carefully chosen as the most suitable and oldest
Orkney word I know' (*The Scottish Antiquary*
8.53). The corollary holds true: wherever the
dialect words (rather than dialect forms) are
thin on the ground, the line is likely to be
genuine and not added by Dennison. His picture
of the linguistic history of Orkney is over-
simplified: Norn ballads were current in North
Ronaldsay about 1770 (see Hugh Marwick, *The
Orkney Norn*, London 1929, p.227, quoting Scott)
and may still have been being composed or added
to in one island while our Scots ballad was
circulating in others or even among the same
people. (A similar situation between Gaelic and
Scots or English is to be found in some bilingual regions today, with some local bards
actually ready to compose songs in either language.) But the hybrid, basically Scots dialect
of the 'peasantry' was not apparently used for
poetry until recent times, with the possible
exception of the New Year Song, 'St.Mary's Men',
and did not even influence the vocabulary of
imported Scots songs much in the course of oral
transmission.

21 It seems that in B she is already married (to
the gunner). But possibly Dennison's amplification of this detail into the basis of much of
his poem draws on some different traditional
tale, though his crusader setting smacks more
of Ivanhoe that Earl Rognvald.

22 *Aloor!* (alas) and *büddo* (darling) are often
used by Dennison — though admittedly they were
not uncommon features in the spoken dialect:
the first was certainly used a generation ago
and the second can still be heard from the oldest generation in the North Isles.

23 He notes however (*The Scottish Antiquary* 7.173)
'these periods were a subject of dispute among
my oral authorities', and Keillor in his MSS
accompanying B (NLS 50. I. 13 f. 324^V) gives it
as the North Ronaldsay belief that seals could
become men and women at every *ninth* stream tide.

24 'Mester' in the sense of 'mighty' is no doubt
original in the titles of the traditional tales
of 'The Mester Ship' and 'Assipattle and the
Mester Stoorworm' given by Dennison (*The Scottish Antiquary* 5.68, 130) but again it is a word
which he evidently liked and used as much as
possible.

25 A minimum of adaptation is needed from the
sound of 'Ogilvie' to 'Odivere' and from 'kiss
me fairly' to 'see me farly fang' — *i.e.*'see my
wonderful catch'.

26 This is surely metaphor rather than actual
belief: salt is usually invoked *against* supernatural beings and their magic, for instance to
capture the vanishing isle of Eynhallow (*The
Scottish Antiquary* 7.117-20), and many Orcadians must have known that it was possible to

shoot ordinary seals in or by salt water. The
usual form of the belief is illustrated from
North Ronaldsay in another passage from Keillor's MS (f.323ᵛ): a man shooting rabbits by
night saw a strange pony which he decided must
be Tangie (the Orkney sea-kelpie). He could not
shoot it until he put a sixpence in the gun;
then it fell, and he left the body on the shore
to be carried out by the tide.

27 Charles Thomson's MS consists of three folded
sheets: the ballad is on both sides of the
sixth leaf and is clearly intended to be part
of the collection. But it is written in a hand
barely recognisable as the neat if rather
crabbed script in which the rest of the MS
(containing the well-known tale of the Goodman
of Westness and his seal bride) is written: in
the accompanying letter he asks Keillor to
transcribe his MS in a better hand, and must, I
think, have meant the ballad in particular.
There is no punctuation at all and the use of
capitals is eccentric. In fact it looks rather
like Campbell of Islay's own notes made in the
field, and it seems very likely that the ballad
was written down directly from the dictation or
more probably singing of Thomson's informant,
not retold in his own words like the accompanying tale. Thomson might incidentally be the
educated North Ronaldsay source for Dennison's
version of the latter (*The Scottish Antiquary*
7.173), so he *may* also be one of his sources
for the ballad.

28 This is not to say that his ballad is artistic-
ally more acceptable: in five verses, three of
them apparently entirely genuine, the second
line virtually repeats the first in a way which
adds nothing to the effect. Possibly 'the very

first shot' in B 11 is simply deduced from B 7
c, the line corresponding to A 7 c, but if so
'very' has dropped out there in our text.

29 David Buchan, *The Ballad and the Folk* (London,
1972) pp.51-173.

30 This seems probable on empirical grounds, since
if other singers always improvised slightly
differently it would be impossible to learn the
ballad word-for-word by listening to successive
performances: it would be necessary to perfect
one's own improvised version to learn. Parallels from Gaelic prose storytelling support
this: in Gaelic tales the narrative is usually
told in the teller's own words, but dialogue
and descriptive passages in the more formal
heroic tales are often learned by heart and repeated almost word-for-word each time the story
is told. A comparison of different recordings
of the same tale from the South Uist story-
tellers Duncan MacDonald and Angus MacLellan
shows that both of them did this, but Duncan
repeated certain of his father's tales word-for-
word throughout. One of these, *Conall Gulban*,
was also learned by Angus from Duncan's father,
but told quite differently even in the unvary-
ing 'runs' and dialogue: so Angus's version
must be his own compilation.

31 Scots speakers were in Orkney long before it
passed to the Scottish Crown, but Scots probably only overtook Norn as the language of the
bulk of the people after the beginning of the
seventeenth century (see Hugh Marwick, *The
Orkney Norn*, p.xxiv). I think it is fair to
assume that a ballad in Scots would not have
been made out of a native story before that
date; and this agrees with the period from
which the majority of extant historical ballads

in the classical style seem to date by their subject-matter.

32 'Odivere' has 93 stanzas. Several ballads which were popular in Orkney before 1914, and were actually sung all through, are between half and two-thirds as long: 'Andrew Lammie' (Child 233, which incidentally *was* performed as a play in Orkney not so long ago) has some 55 verses, 'Sir James the Rose' (Child 213, the 'Michael Bruce' text) is equally long, 'The Turkey Factor' has 48 quatrains of longer lines. Typically, though all these three ballads may be of Scottish composition, only the first makes any pretence to be in Scots, and in the long modern version it is much anglicised.

5. *THE GREY COCK*: DAWN SONG OR REVENANT BALLAD?

Hugh Shields

1 This article translates and revises 'Une *alba* dans la poésie populaire anglaise?', a paper read at the sixth *Congrès de langue et littérature d'Oc*, Montpellier 1970, and published in *Revue des langues romanes*, LXXIX (1971) 461-75. Since 1970, the final volume of B.H.Bronson's *Traditional tunes of the Child ballads* has appeared (IV, Princeton 1972, henceforth 'Bronson'), with versions of the *Grey cock* on pp.15-23, and I have discussed the ballad in a general context, 'The dead lover's return in modern English ballad tradition' in *Jahrbuch für Volksliedforschung*, XVII (1972) 98-114, henceforth '*Jahrbuch*'. Though other texts of the ballad have come to my notice, they do not cause me to modify my earlier view that the *Grey cock* began as 'a variety of the *aube*': the

view expressed in the often too sketchy but
rarely misleading or injudicious pages of F.J.
Child, *The English and Scottish popular ballads*,
Boston 1882-98, IV 389-90, henceforth 'Child'.

Folk songs collected by me in Ireland during
the years 1966-72, indexed in *Ulster folklife*,
XXI (1975) 25-54, are referred to by their
number in that index. For the texts of the
ballad studied, see the Appendix below.

2 See T.J.B.Spencer in *Eos. An enquiry into the
theme of lovers' meetings and partings at dawn
in poetry*, ed. A.T.Hatto, The Hague 1965,
pp.505-53 (texts, 532-53); H.Schelp, 'Die Tradition der *Alba* und die Morgenszene in Chaucers
Troilus and Criseyde' in *Germanisch-romanische
Monatsschrift*, XV (1965) 251-61.

3 Recorded H.Shields, no.267 (unpublished?). For
the subject in general see C.R.Baskervill,
'English songs of the night visit' in *Publications of the Modern Language Association*, XXXVI
(1921) 565-614.

4 Typical examples are *Trooper and maid* (Child
299) and *Abroad as I was walking*, see n.38.

5 Friedman, op.cit. in Appendix *A*; *Eos*, p.512;
Child, IV 389-90; Baskervill, op.cit., p.601-
10; Bronson, IV 15-23; *Jahrbuch*, pp.104-5. A
lover's infidelity in texts of the *Grey cock*
($B^{1.6}$, vv.3-4, below) will be discussed later.

6 See nn.49, 56.

7 L.C.Wimberly, *Folklore in the English and Scottish ballads*, 1928, repr. New York 1965, pp.225-
69. Unlike Child, IV 390, and Baskervill, op.
cit., p.601ff., recent writers incline to believe in the revenant: see Friedman, Barry and
Coffin, opera cit, in Appendix B^2, *A*, con-

clusion; M.Dean-Smith, *A guide to English folk-song collections*, Liverpool 1954, pp.24, 71; MacEdward Leach, *The ballad book*, New York and London 1955, p.611.

8 Many songs touch on the theme, but leave us uncertain whether they draw on lost dawn songs, in, for example the allusion to cockcrow as a sign of dawn (*The chickens they are crowing* in C.Sharp, *English folk songs from the Southern Appalachians*, London 1932, II 378) or the declaration, more festive than amorous, that ''tis not day, 'tis not yet day' (*The pitcher* in W.H.Logan, *A pedlar's pack of ballads and songs*, Edinburgh 1869, p.235, cf. Irish *Níl sé ina lá*, discussed by Seán Ó Tuama, *An grá in amhráin na ndaoine*, Dublin 1960, p.71, and Occitanian *D'enquera n'es pas jorn*, see *French folk songs from Corrèze, Chants corréziens*. LP disc and pamphlet ed. H.Shields, Topic records 12 T 246, London 1974). In one American version of *Trooper and maid*, the trooper says 'I hear the rooster crow, And I must be a-goin'', *Frank C.Brown collection of N.Carolina folklore*, II, Durham, N.C., 1952, 199. Among old ballads, more palpable traces of the *alba* are in *Little Musgrave*: lovers converse about daybreak announced by bird song (Child 81 A, II 244) or a well-wisher among the husband's approaching throng warns little Musgrave of their approach by blowing his horn (81 B, II 247).

9 Coll. H.Shields no.86, and ed. from another informant on *Adam in Paradise*, EP disc and pamphlet, Ulster Folk Museum, 1969. Dean-Smith, op.cit. in n.7, gives the song under the titles *Arise, arise, you drowsy maiden*, p.48, and *Oh, who is that raps at my window?*, p.94.

10 Coll. H.Shields no.217.

11 As in *The sweet Bann water*, Henry, op.cit. in
Appendix B^2, no.722; cf. version *r* in note 14.

12 G.Greig, *Folk song of the North East*, repr.
Hatboro, Pa., 1963, no.LIV.

13 It is true that supernatural texts of the *Grey
cock* (D^{2-7}, *E*) agree, awkwardly enough, more
closely with the text of the *Drowsy sleeper*
than do *alba* texts, in which the idea of final
parting is usually expressed by a different
image, 'And seven moons shine brightly o'er yon
lea' ($B^2.4-5$, cf.$B^1.4-6$). Nevertheless, two
alba texts include the first of the two familiar
lines, 'When the fishes they do fly, the
seas they all run dry' ($B^2.5$, cf.$B^2.4$, preceding the line just quoted), so that the absence
of these lines from other *alba* texts can be the
result of accidents of transmission. See below,
at n.58, for further discussion of 'impossibles'.

14 *a*. F.Purslow, *The wanton seed*, London 1969,
p.86; *b*. Greig, op.cit., no.clxxvii; *c*. E.B.
Lyle, *Andrew Crawfurd's collection of ballads
and songs*, I, Edinburgh 1975, p.43; *d*. Bronson, IV
20, no.10; *e*. N.Buchan & P.Hall, *The Scottish
folk singer*, London & Glasgow 1973, p.96;
f. Fowke, op.cit. in Appendix, conclusion, p.
105; *g*. H.Creighton, *Maritime folk songs*, Toronto 1962, p.63. Some of these renditions have
been published on discs. For other unpublished
recordings, see nn.10, 11, 17 (*h-j*); *k*. School
of Scottish Studies SA 1955/15; BBC Archive,
l. RPL 18789 (Scotland), *m*. 18410 (Ireland),
n. 22036 (do.), *o*. 22423 (do.); Dept. of Educa-
tion, Dublin, *p*. 229/1, *q*. 235/3; *r*. sung at
Belfast, 1974, by Tríona Ní Dhónaill, from Co.
Donegal tradition. *s*. See n.22.

[15] Except the version cited in n.17 (*j*). The allusion to cockcrow is in *d*, *f*, *l-p*.

[16] Dean-Smith, op.cit. in n.7, p.24. There is actually no 'star' in the Birmingham text; in v.1 iii, this writer has mis-interpreted 'stumble' as 'star'.

[17] Recorded by T.Munnelly, 1967, from the late John Reilly, Co.Roscommon (unpublished).

[18] Texts mentioning a 'burning tempest' (*a*, *f*, *n*, *o*) are just as lacking in supernatural features as the other texts. The phrase was perhaps a lyric evocation of the lover's emotions. Or could we read 'birring tempest'?— see *birr* 'to commence to blow' etc. in *Scottish National Dictionary* I 136-7 and *OED* I 875. Notice also [Gerard Boate], *A natural history of Ireland in three parts*, Dublin 1726 (first ed. 1652) p.9 (ch.II iv) 'Before the mouth of this lough lieth a great sand, called the Touns (upon which it burneth greatly, when the wind bloweth from the sea)'; the French edition, *Histoire naturelle de l'Irlande*, Paris 1666, p.26, reads 'sur lequel il se fait un grand bruit'.

[19] By H.Creighton, op.cit. in n.14, p.113; G.Wood in *Traditional topics*, I ii (Feb. 1968); H. Shields in *Jahrbuch*, pp.111-4; see also n.66. Addendum: two more versions of *Willy-O*, in Sharon Gmelch, *Tinkers and travellers*, Dublin 1975, p.137, and in *Tocher*, no.19, Edinburgh 1975, pp.104-5, are erroneously identified as versions of the *Grey cock*.

[20] *Jahrbuch* p.113, text *A*, from an Irish broadside of about 1850. A Co.Donegal version is on the LP *Folk ballads from Donegal and Derry*, ed. H. Shields, Leader Sound, LEA 4055, London 1972.

21 See n.17.

22 This expression of parting is also found in another curiously amplified version of *I must
away* which however lacks both the revenant and
the nuclear verses of the *Grey cock*, while on
the other hand it seems to borrow from *Reilly
from the Co.Cavan/Kerry* and perhaps from other
sources — recorded by R.S.Thomson from Eddie
Hayes of Lisselton, Co.Clare, *Let the night be
as dark as dungeon* (Singers' workshop archive,
7b Carlton Drive, London S.W.15, tape England
no.29).

23 *Jahrbuch*, pp.99, 107.

24 *Fair Margaret* has no close textual parallels
with the verse quoted; various revenant ballads
offer what could have been the makings of this
return from the dead. In the broadside *William
and Margaret*, v.13 runs: 'The hungry worm my
sister is; This winding-sheet I wear: And cold
and weary lasts our night, Till that last morn
appear.' — *Roxburghe ballads*, ed. W.Chappell,
III, London 1880, 672; thus verbatim the *'Margaret's ghost'* version made by David Mallet,
see T.Percy, *Reliques of ancient English poetry*,
ed. H.B.Wheatley, 1886, repr. New York, 1966,
III 312. 'Sweet William' (Child 77) brings from
the grave in some versions a holland — or winding — sheet instead of a love token: Bronson II
230, 232 (nos.2, 3, 9); Child, II 231, C;
*Journal of the English Folk Dance and Song
Society*, VIII (1956) 17; in another version he
tells Margaret 'Cold meal is my covering owre,
But an my winding sheet; My bed it is full low,
I say, Down among the hongerey worms I sleep.'
—Child, II 230, B. A similar v. occurs in
Proud lady Margaret (Child 47), where the reven-
ant is the lady's brother: Child, I 427-30,

A-C. Cf. *Romeo and Juliet*, V iii, 109.

25 These texts name the dead girl 'Margaret'; cf. Child 74, 77, and *William and Margaret*.

26 This despite a literary revenant ballad with a male ghost by A.P.Graves, loc.cit. in Appendix F^5, based on 'a fragment' obtained from Joyce and published 27 years before Joyce's traditional text appeared in print. Graves had access only to the four lines that promise a reward to the cock,· which he said derived from 'a ballad descriptive of the visit of a lover's ghost to his betrothed', op.cit., p.249. Graves may have been mistaken; since 1970 I have found no other evidence which might cast a slur on Joyce's fidelity to his source.

27 In this and other respects, *William and Margaret* also draws on *Sweet William's ghost*, reversing the roles. Baskervill, op.cit. in n.3, p.568n, points out the uniqueness of Ophelia's song *Tomorrow is St Valentine's day*, *Hamlet* IV 5, in its suggesting a night visit from a girl to her lover: but of course Ophelia is mad.

28 See H.Shields, 'Old British ballads in Ireland' in *Folklife*, X (1972) 85-6; recorded on the disc mentioned in n.20.

29 For the additional text see W.Montgomerie in *Studies in Scottish literature*, IV (1967) 195.

30 *Vocal music*, pp.36-7, see Appendix B^3. The hemistichs of the odd lines are printed as full lines in this edition, as in many others.

31 The date appears in what seems to be the same hand on the verso of the single leaf.

32 Corrected to *fly up fly up* (*manu 1^a*).

33 Polite editions were extremely numerous; see

Bronson, IV 16, to which may be added British
Museum copies G 800 m (42), London n.d., H 1653
r (6), Edinburgh n.d. (1820s?), H 1224 (33) 'A
favorite Scottish ballad newly arranged...by
Wm.Hawes', London n.d. (1820?), H 296 (3) 'by
Ferd.Ries', n.p.d. (1822?); copies of other un-
noticed editions are in the National Library of
Ireland, Joly 3329, on sheets for *Exshaw's
Gentleman's and London magazine*, n.p.d.(Dublin),
Add.Mus.9957, Benjamin Rhames, Dublin, n.d.
(1790s?), *The charms of melody*, John Colles,
Temple Lane, Dublin 1776, pt.I, p.27, no.lvi.
An English broadside is in Cambridge univ.
library, Madden ballads, VI 1680, publ. by J.
Holloway and J.Black, *Later English broadside
ballads*, London 1975, pp.244-5; a Scottish song
book from which the text is lacking (mentioned
on t.-p.) is in the Bradshaw collection, ibid.,
no.7809, Duncan, Glasgow. Except the last three,
texts are accompanied by the melody (variants
of the melody mentioned below). Texts reproduce
Herd 1776 (B^2) for the most part, but *Charms of
melody* and the English broadside follow *Vocal
music* (B^3).

34 The air served for a poem of Burns, *Where are
the joys I hae met in the morning?*, see *Songs
of Robt.Burns*, ed. J.C.Dick, London etc., 1903,
pp.100, 386-7. Chappell, loc.cit. in Appendix
B^3, attributed it to James Hook. It has not
lasted well in oral tradition; an apparent
Scottish variant was printed in 1866 (Bronson
no.2), and two Co.Antrim versions collected in
the 1930s and in 1975 are adaptations of it
($B^{2.4-5}$). Variants of the eighteenth-century
air have also been attached to songs of successful courtship: see *Cecil Sharp's collection of
English folk songs*, ed. Maud Karpeles, London

1974, I 388-9 'The shepherdess and the sailor',
II 82-3 'The simple ploughboy', cf. I 387 'A
farmer's son so sweet', B melody.

35 Dick, ed. cit., p.387. Parodies or pastiches
included one featuring George Washington, see
Appendix, conclusion; a Methodist hymn, *Saw ye
my Saviour?*, see *Journal of the Folk Song
Society*, VIII no.32 (1928) 79, G.P.Jackson,
Spiritual folk songs of early America, 1937,
repr. New York 1964, pp.44-5, D.Yoder, *Pennsylvania spirituals*, Lancaster, Pa., 1961, pp.11,
358, 427 (reference is made to a German translation of the spiritual), Cambridge univ.
library, Madden ballads, XVIII 1030, Harkness,
Preston, n.d. Textual reminiscences of *Saw you
my father?* occur in *The wee thing, or, Mary of
Castlecary*: Hector MacNeill, *Poetical works*,
Edinburgh 1856, p.82.

36 In Scots /fɔːs : wɔːz/ and in Southern English
/fɔːls : wɔz/. Scotticisms in the Falkirk Muir
MS are: *tirl'd at ye pin* 'rattled the handle',
which becomes in English '*twirled the pin*';
taking tent 'acting cautiously', both better
sense and a better rhyme (*:went*) than English
'*took the hint*'. For other evidence suggesting
Scottish composition see Baskervill, op.cit. in
n.3, p.603n; Jackson, op.cit., p.45.

37 Child, II 232.

38 I have noted it in the *Foggy dew*, see J.Reeves,
The idiom of the people, London 1961 (first ed.
1958), pp.52, 112, and Cambridge univ. library,
Madden ballads, XVI 680; in *Abroad as I was
walking*, Reeves, op.cit. in Appendix A^4, p.41,
and op.cit. sup., p.107, Purslow, op.cit. in
n.14, p.6, Dean-Smith, op.cit. in n.7, '*The
squire and the fair maid*', p.107, Karpeles, op.

cit. in Appendix D^5 (1971 ed.) p.208.

39 Friedman, op.cit. in Appendix A^1, p.287; Chappell, op.cit. in Appendix B^3, I 58. A similar lyric formula occurs in *Searching for lambs*, Reeves, *Idiom*, p.193, 'But I'd rather be in my true love's arms Than any other where'.

40 Text: *Exetnsis*.

41 *Tirry-Cock*: '?'. 'Thristle-cock' (thrush) is not apt, and *tarrock*, var. *tirrick*, 'sea bird', Scots, is both inept and dialectally remote; *tirry* 'ill natured', Shet. and Ork., though apt, is still more remote. Probably the best interpretation is 'singing cock', on the analogy of *tirra-lirra*, 'refrain, or, birdsong (especially of the lark)'. Bold's Latin does not render *tirry*; later texts omit it or give an easier reading: pretty ($A^{2,4}$), wonderful (A^5).

42 Friedman, op.cit. in Appendix A^1, p.289.

43 In the *Jolly beggar* for example (Child 279) 'When twenty weeks were over she looked most pale and wan', Bronson IV 223, no.29. 'Wan' as the heroine's surname in the oldest text of *Lizzie Wan* (Child 51, I 448) may have been suggested by the fact of her pregnancy. At any rate, pallor is a motif symbolic of pregnancy in many ballads. For *Willy of Winsbury* see n.46.

44 *Young Johnny was a ploughboy*, Reeves, op.cit. in Appendix A^4, p.281.

45 *Loose and humorous songs from bishop Percy's folio MS*, ed. F.J.Furnivall, repr. Hatboro, Pa., & London, 1963, p.55.

46 In *Willy of Winsbury* (Child 100) a father asks his daughter if she looks 'pale and wan' from sickness or because a young man has deceived

her (understand, left her with child); but she
tells him the reason is that her 'true love
stops too long' away, see *Folklife*, art. cit.
in n.28, p.95. In 1617, Thomas Campion wrote
'Maids are full of longing thoughts that breed
a bloodless sickness', see J.Wardroper, *Love
and drollery*, London 1969, p.49. Lascivious
widows too could be 'wan an' pale', see *Tweed-
mouth town* in R.Burns, *The merry muses of
Caledonia*, London 1965, p.195. And the description of love-making in pastourelles often
mentions the girl's 'changing colours', 'with
flashes changeing pale and red' etc., see
Purslow, op.cit. in Appendix A^5, p.48; H.
Shields, 'Some "Songs and Ballads in use in the
Province of Ulster...1845": Texts', in *Ulster
folklife*, XVIII (1972) 65; Wardroper, op.cit.,
p.231.

47 See *Journal of the Folk Song Society*, VIII
no.34 (1930) 200; W.H.Gill, *Manx national songs*,
London 1896, pp.93-5.

48 Except that A^3 includes the promise but omits
the deception, drawn no doubt from *Saw you my
father?*, still fashionable in 1827.

49 E.Rolland, *Recueil de chansons populaires*,
Paris 1883-90, IV 44; in other texts the cock
replaces the skylark; see ib., and P.Coirault,
Formation de nos chansons folkloriques, I,
Paris 1953, 159-60, A.Jeanroy, *Les origines de
la poésie lyrique en France au moyen âge*, Paris
1904 (first ed. 1889), pp.69-70, *Romania*, VII
(1878), 56-8, *Eos* (see n.2), pp.350, 356-7, 370.

50 The rewards promised to these talking birds,
and to the Grey Cock of our ballad, have a
lyric parallel in fifteenth-century French, *Le
joly gay*, see G.Paris & A.Gevaert, *Chansons du*

quinziéme siècle, Paris 1875, pp.29-30, musical
appendix p.15. The escaped tame bird of the
French poem is an evident symbol of lost vir-
ginity, '...Reviens, reviens, mon joly gay
Dedans ta gabiole, D'or et d'argent la te feray
Dedans comme dehors.' For a discussion of the
'bird-soul' in ballads see Wimberly, op.cit. in
n.7, pp.44-52.

51 Baskervill, op.cit. in n.3, p.602, suggests the
ballad is of the mid-fifteenth century at least,
on the evidence of a regrettably brief quota-
tion 'Cok craw thow quhill day' given as the
title of a dance in the Scots *Tale of Colkelbie
sow*; see *The Bannatyne Manuscript* Vol.IV ed.
W.Tod Ritchie (Scottish Text Society, Edinburgh,
1930) p.291, l. 303.

52 Barry et al., op.cit. in Appendix $B^{2.3}$, p.313.

53 In the *Nonne Preestes Tale*, see Baskervill,
p.609.

54 R.H.Robbins, *Secular lyrics of the fourteenth
and fifteenth centuries*, Oxford 1955, p.41;
repr. *Eos* (see n.2) p.539.

55 For discussion of cockcrow and revenants see
Wimberly, op.cit. in n.7, pp.248-53, and *Jahrbuch*, pp.103-4.

56 'Il n'est mie jours, saverouze au cors gent;
Si m'aït amors, l'alowette nos mant', *It is not
day at all, sweet, fine-bodied one; May love
help me, the lark is lying to us*, K.Bartsch,
Altfranzösische Romanzen und Pastourellen,
Leipzig 1870, pp.27-8 and notes; cf. Jeanroy,
op.cit. in n.49, p.68.

57 *The drowsy sleeper*, see n.12.

58 It would be another day's work to show, as I

suspect to be the case, that impossibles of the
type 'When fishes fly' = 'never' were proper in
early times, not to the language of revenant
ballads, but to that of ballads and songs concerned with earthly affairs: in particular,
with love and infidelity and with the lyric
rather than narrative treatment of such affairs.
For the present, it can be noted that neither
in Child nor in Bronson do we meet any revenant
ballads — apart from the revenant texts of the
Grey cock we have examined — in which such
hyperbole is used, whereas flying fishes,
mussels growing on trees, cockle shells that
turn to silver bells, seas that go dry, sun and
moon leaping or dancing, trees dripping wine,
occur plentifully in ballads with no supernatural element: Child nos.13, (Bronson *1-5, 6b,
12, 14-7, 19, 21-2, 3.1, 3.2*), 49D-F, I (and
Bronson *41, 10.1*) 51AB (and Bronson *2-4, 5b,
6*), 204 introd., A-D, F-M (and Bronson *8*), 218B
(and Bronson *2-4*), 299A-D (and Bronson *5, 8-10,
12, 16, 17, 19-21, 24-7*).

It is noteworthy that some texts of the
lyric version (A^{3-5}) end with a strong expression of the lover's *fidelity*, which appears
earlier (1827) than the hyperbole for infidelity (1916). It almost seems as if a strong expression of one sort or the other has come to
be felt as necessary to round off the dawn
parting.

59 Another impossible appropriate to earthly rather
than unearthly doings; cf. *Rosemary lane*, 'She
wished that long (*read* short) night had been
seven long year', in Reeves, op.cit. in Appendix A^4, p.223, and Old French 'Adonc vocex-
iens nous lai ke celle nut durest sant' in the
poem cited in n.56: *Then we would have wished
that night to last [as long as] a hundred.*

60 Plainly observable in A^3.

61 See *Jahrbuch*.

62 L.Vargyas, *Researches into the mediaeval history of folk ballad*, Budapest 1967, pp.258-9.

63 Represented in the Appendix by what must be understood in some cases as quite approximate grouping.

64 For example, both *alba* and revenant texts may make opening mention of weather ($B^{1.2-5}$, $B^{2}.4-5$, C, D^{2-4}) or of a girl's solitude ($B^{1.2-3}$, $B^{2}.4-5$, D^{2-3}, 5), or they may omit such mention; or the return to the girl's bed may be similarly mentioned (A^{1}, ^{4}, $B^{1}.4-5$, C, D^{4-5}) or omitted.

65 In Bronson's group A^{b}, *4* and *5* are clearly related, as are *6* and *7*; *3* shows slight agreement with *14* (= group *B*), especially in its fourth phrase. In group A^{c}, *12* and *13* agree closely; *11* on the other hand agrees with *16* ('group *C*'), and their similarity is underlined if we refer to the variant cadence for *16* noted from another rendition by the same singer, in *Penguin book of English folk songs*, loc.cit. in Appendix *E*. Group *C* seems a non-starter; its two members, *15, 16*, seem unrelated to each other, and *15*, publ. without text under the title '*The Song of the ghost*', is closer to tunes of *Sweet William's ghost* (cf. Bronson, II 232-3, nos.7-11, and R.Morton, *Folk songs sung in Ulster*, Cork 1970, p.12) than to tunes of the *Grey cock*.
Tunes not in Bronson might be related to those he includes as follows: $B^{1.6}$ is the first half of '*Lazarus/Job*' and as such related to the opening of no.*8*. $B^{2.2}$, which seems badly notated, approaches *11-13* most closely. $B^{2.4-5}$ agree in their lines i, iv, with group A^{a}, but

in lines ii-iii with group A^C (no.*8*). D^4 resembles other tunes of similar provenance (Nova
Scotia):*12, 13*.

66 So for example Bronson includes versions of
Willy-O (for which the title *'Fly up, my cock'*
is erroneous) and *I must away* among melodic
variants of the *Grey cock* (nos.*9, 10*).

67 Dr R.S.Thomson tells me that he expects to put
this project in hand.

APPENDIX: TEXTS OF THE *GREY COCK* USED IN THIS
          ARTICLE

Titles are given only if they seem likely to have
had some traditional status. In adopting Herd's
title *'The Grey cock'* Child may have done us a
disservice. As in most other texts, the girl in
Herd promises the cock wings (*var.* comb, neck) of
the 'silver grey': a rather paltry offering if the
cock is already a grey one, which he is in the
eighteenth-century *B* versions and texts influenced
by them ($B^2.2-3$, $F2,4$). The rest of texts show a
wonderful diversity of epithets: little tirry A^1,
pretty crowing A^4, wonderful A^5, bonny $B^{1.3}$, well
feathered $B^{1.6}$, pretty little A^2, $B^{2.4-5}$, bonny,
bonny F^1, pretty...handsome F^5, braw little C,
pretty pretty...handsome little D^1, false crowing
D^3. Some suppress the word *cock*, though the
rooster happily does not appear, and the epithet
grey does not recur: ye bird of early dawn, O ye
well feathered bird (*!*) $B^{1.2}$, pretty feathered
fowls $B^{1.4-5}$, pretty crowing chicken F^3, pretty
little cockerel...very handsome cockerel D^2,
pretty little cuckoo D^4, my little bird D^5, birds
D^6, handsome cockerel E.

A 1 Printed 1685 in Henry Bold, *Latine Songs, with
their English: and Poems*, London, pp.44-9, no
title; repr. A.B.Friedman, *'The Grey cock* — a
drollery version' in *Journal of American folklore*, LXVII (1954) 285-90, see pp.286-7, and
above.

2 Broadside, 1750-95, in Cambridge univ. lib.,
Madden ballads, V 1238, n.p.d., 'A new love
song'.

3 Printed 1827 by T.Lyle, *Ancient ballads and
songs*, London, pp.142-3, 'The swain's resolve',
noted mainly in Glasgow.

4 Noted Dorset 1905, text in J.Reeves, *The everlasting circle*, London 1960, pp.136-7 ('A').

5 Noted as *4*, text in op.cit., pp.137-8 ('B');
text and melody in *Journal of the Folk Song
Society*, VIII no.34 (1930) 199-201, 'Oh, once
I loved a lass', J.Brocklebank & B.Kindersley,
A Dorset book of folk songs, London 1948, p.7,
and Bronson (no.14); F.Purslow, *The Marrow
Bones*, London 1965, p.52, conflates texts 4
and 5. See also n.47.

B MS dated 'Falkirk Muir 6 Septr. 1768', Scottish
Record Office, Edinburgh, RH 13/40, printed
above.

B^1 1 Printed 1769 by D.Herd, *The ancient and modern Scots songs*, Edinburgh, p.324; cf. Child,
IV 390.

2 Learnt Co.Derry, 1900s, by H.Hughes, text and
melody printed in his *Irish country songs*, II,
London 1915, 64-9, 'The light of the moon'
and in Bronson (no.8). BBC 22336, 'The light
of the moon', sung by John McLaverty, Belfast,
in 1952, obviously derives from this published version.

3 Text noted Co.Mayo, 1936, Folklore Dept.,
University College, Dublin, MS 248, p.162.

4 Noted N.Carolina 1916, text and melody in
O.Campbell & C.Sharp, *English folk songs from
the Southern Appalachians*, New York & London
1917, pp.128-9, 2nd ed. 1932, I 259-60, and
in Bronson (no.6); text repr. in *Eos* (see n.2)
p.538.

5 Recorded N.Carolina 1948, from the daughter
of the preceding singer, text and melody in
Bronson (no.7).

6 Recorded Co.Antrim 1955 by Seán Ó Baoill, BBC
24835, text and melody above.

B^2 1 Printed 1776 by D.Herd, *Ancient and modern
Scottish songs*, Edinburgh, II 208; inter-
polated text of $B^{1.1}$, often repr., cf. Child,
IV 390 and Bronson (no.1); see also n.33.

2 Noted Oklahoma, 1960s, text (nearly identical
with $B^{2.1}$) and melody in E. & C.O.Moore,
Ballads and folk songs of the South-West,
Norman, Oklahoma, 1964, pp.113-5.

3 Noted Maine, 1928, text (nearly identical
with $B^{2.1}$) in Phillips Barry, F.H.Eckstorm &
M.W.Smyth, *British ballads from Maine*, New
Haven 1929, pp.310-3.

4 Noted Co.Antrim, 1930s, text and sol-fa
melody in S.Henry, *Songs of the people*, type-
script/offprint collection in National
Library, Dublin and elsewhere, no.699 'The
bonny bushes bright'.

5 Recorded Co.Derry 1975 by H.Shields from two
Co.Antrim informants.

B^3 Printed 1771?, text and melody, in *Vocal music;
or, the Songster's Companion*, Robt.Horsfield,
22 Ludgate St., London, n.d., vol.II of the
series?, pp.36-7 'Saw you my father?'; repr.
(from this ed. or a later one?) by W.Chappell,
Popular music of the olden time, London 1855-9,
II 731; often repr., see n.33.

C Noted N.-E. Scotland, early nineteenth century,
text forming the first half of *Willy's fatal
visit* (Child 255, IV 415-6), in P.Buchan,
*Ancient ballads and songs of the North of Scot-
land*, Edinburgh 1828, II 259-60.

D 1 Learnt Limerick, 1840s, by P.W.Joyce and
published, text and melody, in his *Old Irish
folk music and songs*, Dublin & London 1909,
p.219, 'The lover's ghost'; repr. Bronson
(no.12), Barry & al., op.cit. at $B^{2.3}$ (text
only), p.312, and *Eos*, see n.2 (text only),
p.539. A literary refection and a closely
agreeing melody were printed by W.B.Yeats &
F.R.Higgins on a Cuala broadside, Dublin,
1935?; see also F^5 below, and the rendition by
John Goodluck on *The Suffolk miracle*, Tradition TSR 015, 1974.

2 Noted Nova Scotia, 1930s, text and melody in
H.Creighton & D.Senior, *Traditional ballads
from Nova Scotia*, Toronto 1950, pp.83-4,
'Margaret and John' ('A'), and in Bronson
(no.11).

3 Noted, published and titled as 2, Creighton &
Senior, pp.84-5 ('B'), Bronson no.13.

4 Recorded Nova Scotia 1949, by Helen Creighton
from Amos Jollimore, National Museum of Man,
Ottawa, reel 24/4.

5 Noted Newfoundland 1929 by Maud Karpeles, text
and melody in her *Folk songs from Newfoundland*,
London 1971, pp.100-1, 'The lover's ghost'
('A'), notes on pp.271-2; repr. Bronson (no.5);
see next item.

6 Noted, published and titled as 5, Karpeles,
pp.101-2 ('B'), notes on pp.271-2; repr. Bronson (no.3); M.Karpeles, *Folk songs from Newfoundland*, London 1934, pp.107-10, is a conflated text of 5 and 6.

7 Noted as *5*, lv. and melody publ. Bronson (no. 4). For an unconsulted Canadian recording, see below.

E Recorded Birmingham 1951, BBC 17031, text and melody in *Journal of the English Folk-Dance and Song Society*, VII no.2 (1953) 97-8, 'The lover's ghost', repr. Bronson (no.16); text partly given above, recording (vv.1-3) on the LP disc *Folk songs of Britain*, V, Topic records 12 T 161, London 1969; melody and adapted text in R.V. Williams & A.L.Lloyd, *The Penguin book of English folk songs*, London 1959, pp.52-3.

F Interpolated or isolated fragments:
1 Ireland? 1787?, text of 2vv. in *Notes and queries*, 1st ser.VI (1852) 227; cf. op.cit., 6th ser.XII (1885) 223-5.
2 Scotland, noted 1830, text of 3vv. incorporated into the *Broomfield hill* (Child 43 E, I 399).
3 N.Carolina, mid-twentieth century, lv. prefixed to a version of *Lady Isabel and the elf knight* (Child 4), text and melody in Bronson, I 95-6.
4 Printed 1810, lv. of 8 ll. incorporated into a literary adaptation put forth as traditional (by Allan Cunningham?), in R.H.Cromek, *Remains of Nithsdale and Galloway song*, London, pp.74-5.
5 Printed 1880, lv. obtained from P.W.Joyce (see *D¹*) and used in a literary text, 'The song of the ghost', by A.P.Graves in his *Irish songs and ballads*, Manchester, pp.50-2, 222, 249, repr. in his *Irish song book*, London etc., 1897, p.21; the air is Petrie's '*Song of the ghost*', publ. by Bronson as no.15 (see n.65 above).

I have not been able to obtain the recording
sung by Nina Bartley Finn, mentioned as in the
Library of Congress by Creighton & Senior, op.cit.
at D^2, p.83, or to consult the Isaiah Thomas collection, Worcester, Mass., III 50, mentioned by T.
Coffin, *The British ballad in N.America*, Philadelphia 1963, p.139, as having a version of the
Grey cock. But Coffin is evidently mis-represent-
ing a parody of the ballad, *Saw you my Hero,
George?*, featuring George Washington in events of
the year 1778: see W.C.Ford, 'The Isaiah Thomas
collection of ballads' in *Proceedings of the
American Antiquarian Society*, new ser., XXXIII
(1924), 92, no.235. '*I'll go see my love*' in Edith
Fowke, *Traditional singers and songs from Ontario*,
Hatboro, Pa., 1965, p.105, notes on p.185, is a
version of the song *I must away* (see n.14 above).

For documents and other assistance with this
article I am very grateful to Miss Marie Slocombe
and Miss Madeau Stewart (BBC), Dr Maud Karpeles
(London), Dr Carmen Roy (National Museum of Man,
Ottowa), Mr Tom Munnelly (University College,
Dublin), Mr Seán Ó Baoill (Armagh), Dr R.S.Thomson
(Queens' College, Cambridge), Prof.D.K.Wilgus
(Univ. of California, Los Angeles). Text *B* is
published by permission of the Scottish Record
Office and text $B^{1.6}$ by permission of the BBC.

6. MISS REBURN'S BALLADS

   Alisoun Gardner-Medwin

[1] *Child Waters* (63) in Number 11; *Young Johnstone*
   (88) in Number 32; *Queen Eleanor's Confession*
   (156) in Number 60; *Edom o' Gordon* (178) in
   Number 48; *Sir James the Rose* (213) in Number 30.

2 *Danmarks gamle Folkeviser* edited by Svend
  Grundtvig and others, Copenhagen, 1853-1965,
  II, 57-63.

3 London, 1801, I, 56-60.

4 Number 19.

5 *Reliques of Ancient English Poetry*, Dover
  edition, New York, 1966, I, 143-147.

6 Number 643 in the *Catalogue of English and
  American Chapbooks and Broadside Ballads in
  Harvard College Library, Library of Harvard
  University Bibliographical Contributions*, No.56,
  compiled by Charles Welsh and William H.Tilling-
  hast, Cambridge, Massachusetts, 1905.

7 *Last Leaves of Aberdeenshire Ballads*, collected
  by Gavin Greig and edited by Alexander Keith,
  Aberdeen, 1925. See also Child, *English and
  Scottish Popular Ballads*, III, 423-425 and the
  closing paragraphs of David Buchan's 'History
  and Harlaw' in this book.

8 F.J.Child, *English and Scottish Ballads*, Boston,
  1859, VII, 283.

9 Number 465 in Welsh and Tillinghast *Catalogue*.
  See also numbers 466, 468 and 469.

10 *The Lady of the Lake*, Edinburgh, 1810, in the
   notes to Canto the 4th, stanza VI.

11 Number 936 in Welsh and Tillinghast *Catalogue*.

12 Gavin Greig, *Folk-Song of the North-East*, reprinted by Kenneth Goldstein and Arthur Argo,
   Folklore Associates, Hatboro', Pennsylvania,
   1963, Number 118.

[13] *Irish Texts Society*, University of London, 1908, III, 179-183.

[14] London, 1589, 113.

[15] *American Balladry from British Broadsides*, The American Folklore Society, Philadelphia, 1957, 189-190. A text may be found in C.H.Firth, *An American Garland*, Oxford, 1915, 69-71.

[16] *Journal of the Folk Song Society* II (1905-6), 253; III (1907), 26-31; V, 180. F.Kidson, *English Peasant Songs*, London, 1929, 28. H.Hughes, *Irish Country Songs*, III, London, 1835, 22-25. V.Duffy, *Ballad Poetry of Ireland*, Dublin, 1866, 39th ed., 117. P.W.Joyce, *Old Irish Folk Music and Songs*, London, 1909, 236-7. A.Moffatt, *Minstrelsy of Ireland*, 4th ed., London, 1897, 104. A.P.Graves, *The Catalogue of the Bradshaw Collection*, III, Cambridge, 1914, no.1380. Two possible translations into Irish: M.Hannagan S.Clandillon, *Londubh a chairn*, London, 1927, no.18; Liam de Noraidh, *Ceol o'n Munhan*, Dublin, 1965, 18. *Journal of American Folklore*, xxxv, 202-204, with a bibliography. Cecil Sharp and Maud Karpeles, *English Folk-Songs from the Southern Appalachians*, Oxford University Press, 1932, II, 50. H.M.Belden, *Ballads and Songs*, *University of Missouri Studies*, no.10, 1940, 281-282. V.Randolph, *Ozark Folksongs*, Columbia, Missouri, 1946-50, III, 606. I am indebted to Dr Hugh Shields, Trinity College, Dublin, for some of the Irish references.

[17] See Lockhart's *Life of Scott*, Edinburgh, 1837, V, 306.

[18] Joyce, *Old Irish Folk Music and Songs*, 236.

[19] *Journal of the Folk Song Society*, III, 1907, 30.

20 Bertrand H.Bronson, *The Traditional Tunes of the Child Ballads*, Princeton, 1959-1972, II, 515-529.

21 Greig and Keith, *Last Leaves*, 83-84. See also Bronson, *Traditional Tunes*, II, 521, no.13.

22 See James Reeves, *The Everlasting Circle*, London, 1960; Algirdas Landsbergis and Clark Mills, *The Green Linden*, New York, 1964. I would like to thank Dr David E.Bynum of Harvard for allowing me to audit his lectures in which he discussed this motif.

23 Bronson, *Traditional Tunes*, II, 60.

24 See A.G.Gilchrist, *Journal of the English Folk Dance and Song Society*, I, 1932, 1-17 and Child, *English and Scottish Popular Ballads*, III, 515.

25 Child, *Ballads*, III, 372-376.

26 Bronson, *Traditional Tunes*, I, 143, *The Two Sisters*, examples 72 and 82-86.

27 Andrew Crawfurd's *Auld Ballats*, Paisley Central Library, PC 1453-5, I.125; recorded by Thomas Macqueen in 1827.

28 *The Ballad as Song*, University of California Press, 1969, 64-78.

29 Letter 3, see above p.94.

30 See my article 'The Ancestry of "The House-Carpenter"' in the *Journal of American Folklore*, LXXXIV, 1971, 414-427.

31 The importance of print in the transmission of ballads has recently been reaffirmed by Dr R.S. Thomson's thesis *The Ballad Trade and English Folksong* (unpublished Ph.D. dissertation, Cambridge, 1974).

7. THE SCOTTISH ELEMENT IN AMERICAN BALLADS

Herschel Gower

[1] See also T.J.Wertenbaker, *Early Scotch Contributions to the United States* (Glasgow, 1945); John H.Finley, *The Coming of the Scot* (New York, 1940); J.P.Maclean, *An Historical Account of the Settlements of Scotch Highlanders in America Prior to the Peace of 1783* (Cleveland, 1900); and Duane Meyer, *The Highland Scots of North Carolina* (Chapel Hill, 1961).

[2] The two works most often consulted are: Charles A.Hanna, *The Scotch-Irish; or, The Scot in North Britain, North Ireland, and North America* (New York, 1902); and Henry Jones Ford, *The Scotch-Irish in America* (Princeton, N.J., 1915). Supplementing Hanna and Ford are: Wayland F. Dunaway, *The Scotch-Irish of Colonial Pennsylvania* (Chapel Hill, 1944); and A.J.McKelway, 'The Scotch-Irish of North Carolina', *North Carolina Booklet*, IV, No.11 (March 1905), 3-24. See also the various publications of the Scotch-Irish Society of America.

[3] Howard F.Baker, *National Stocks in the Population of the United States as Indicated by the Surnames in the Census of 1790*. Annual Report of the American Historical Association (Washington, D.C.: Government Printing Office, 1932), p.307.

[4] *Idem.*

[5] *Ibid.*, pp.230-231.

[6] *Ibid.*, pp.256-270.

[7] *Ibid.*, p.231.

[8] *Idem.*

9 *Ibid.*, p.307.

10 See Plate 82 in Charles O.Paullin, *Atlas of the Historical Geography of the United States* (Washington, D.C.: The Carnegie Institution, 1932).

11 Charles W.Dunn, *Highland settler* (Toronto, 1953), pp.13, 27, 74, 79, 138.

12 Carl Wittke, *We Who Made America* (New York, 1940), p.55.

13 Hugh Talmage Lefler and Albert Ray Newsome, *North Carolina* (Chapel Hill, 1954), pp.77-79.

14 Wittke, *op.cit.*, p.59.

15 Constance Rourke, *American Humor* (New York, 1955), p.41.

16 *Marmion*, Canto III, Strophe IX.

17 As quoted in Claude M.Newlin, 'Dialects of the Western Pennsylvania Frontier', *American Speech*, IV (1928-1929), 104.

18 See H.H.Brackenridge, *Modern Chivalry* (Pittsburgh, 1819), II, 4. The author was born near Campbeltown, Scotland, where he lived until his parents took him to America at the age of five. Thereafter, he was brought up in a Scots-Irish community in the southern part of York County, Pennsylvania

19 H.M.Brackenridge, *Recollections of Persons and Places in the West* (Philadelphia, 1868), p.53.

20 Josiah H.Combs, 'Language of the Southern Highlands', *PMLA*, XLVI (1931), 1302-1322. See also Lester V.Berrey, 'Southern Mountain Speech', *American Speech*, XV (1940), 45-46. The author wishes to acknowledge here the helpful notes

and suggestions of Dr Joyce Collie formerly of
the Scottish National Dictionary, Edinburgh.

21 Sir Walter Scott to Archibald Constable, Febru-
ary 25, 1822, in *The Letters of Sir Walter
Scott*, edited by H.J.C.Grierson (London, 1934),
VII, 82-83.

22 Kittredge discusses the contemplated preface
which Child intended, *English and Scottish
Popular Ballads*, Cambridge Edition, p.xxix.

23 It is obviously impossible to deal with all the
analogues in other national literatures or the
many European and Asian stories having points
in common with Scottish ballads. The aim here
is to define the Scottish. ballads in the Child
collection and distinguish them from the English.

24 An indispensable aid in locating the American
texts of Scottish ballads is Tristram P.Coffin,
The British Traditional Ballad in North America
(Philadelphia, 1950; 2nd edn., 1963).

25 For detailed analyses and discussions of the
Scottish 'character' of each ballad listed, see
the author's unpublished doctoral dissertation,
'Traditional Scottish Ballads in the United
States', Vanderbilt University, 1957.

26 For a complete list that also includes songs,
see A.F.Falconer, editor, *The Percy Letters*
(Baton Rouge, 1954), p.xxi. Two publications by
William Walker touch on the subject of separat-
ing English and Scottish ballads: *Peter Buchan
and Other Papers* (Aberdeen, 1915); and *Letters
on Scottish Ballads from Professor Francis J.
Child to W.W.* [William Walker] (Aberdeen:
privately printed at the Bon Accord Press, 1930).

27 Arthur Kyle Davis, Jr., *Traditional Ballads of Virginia* (Chapel Hill, 1960), *passim*.

28 Phillips Barry, *British Ballads from Maine* (New Haven, 1929), pp.303-304.

29 Josiah H.Combs, *Folk-Songs du Midi des Etats-Unis* (Paris, 1925), p.145.

30 Collected by Claude H.Elred at Lake Mills, Wisconsin, in December, 1906, and sung to him by Mrs McLeod of Dumfries, Scotland. *Journal of American Folklore*, XX (April-June 1907), 156.

31 Unpublished MSS of Cecil Sharp, Clare College Library, Cambridge.

32 But it must be remembered that Child's four versions and a fragment were all from Scottish sources, none from English.

33 Edwin Capers Kirkland, '"Sir Patrick Spens" Found in Tennessee', *Southern Folklore Quarterly*, I (December 1937), 1-2.

34 Combs, *op.cit.*, pp.129-133.

35 Helen Hartness Flanders and Marguerite Olney, *Ballads Migrant in New England* (New York, 1953), pp.96-97. Note the version of 'John of Hazelgreen' on page 237:

    'My father is dead and my mother's alive
        But I value it not *a pin*,
    I am weeping for my own true love,
        Young Johnny of Hazel*green*.'

Here the Scottish *preen* has become *pin*. In the version of 'Mary Hamilton' on pages 79-80, *kirk-yard, gowans*, and *rowans* have been retained.

36 Vol.II (Princeton, N.J., 1962), p.428.

37 Tristram P.Coffin, *op.cit.*, *passim*.